Disclosing Protective Services Information

A Guide for North Carolina Social Services Agencies

2015

Aimee N. Wall

UNC
SCHOOL OF
GOVERNMENT

The School of Government at the University of North Carolina at Chapel Hill works to improve the lives of North Carolinians by engaging in practical scholarship that helps public officials and citizens understand and improve state and local government. Established in 1931 as the Institute of Government, the School provides educational, advisory, and research services for state and local governments. The School of Government is also home to a nationally ranked graduate program in public administration and specialized centers focused on information technology and environmental finance.

As the largest university-based local government training, advisory, and research organization in the United States, the School of Government offers up to 200 courses, webinars, and specialized conferences for more than 12,000 public officials each year. In addition, faculty members annually publish approximately 50 books, manuals, reports, articles, bulletins, and other print and online content related to state and local government. Each day that the General Assembly is in session, the School produces the *Daily Bulletin Online*, which reports on the day's activities for members of the legislature and others who need to follow the course of legislation.

The Master of Public Administration Program is offered in two formats. The full-time, two-year residential program serves up to 60 students annually. In 2013 the School launched MPA@UNC, an online format designed for working professionals and others seeking flexibility while advancing their careers in public service. The School's MPA program consistently ranks among the best public administration graduate programs in the country, particularly in city management. With courses ranging from public policy analysis to ethics and management, the program educates leaders for local, state, and federal governments and nonprofit organizations.

Operating support for the School of Government's programs and activities comes from many sources, including state appropriations, local government membership dues, private contributions, publication sales, course fees, and service contracts. Visit www.sog.unc.edu or call 919.966.5381 for more information on the School's courses, publications, programs, and services.

Michael R. Smith, DEAN
Thomas H. Thornburg, SENIOR ASSOCIATE DEAN
Frayda S. Bluestein, ASSOCIATE DEAN FOR FACULTY DEVELOPMENT
Johnny Burleson, ASSOCIATE DEAN FOR DEVELOPMENT
Todd A. Nicolet, ASSOCIATE DEAN FOR OPERATIONS
Bradley G. Volk, ASSOCIATE DEAN FOR ADMINISTRATION

FACULTY

Whitney Afonso	Norma Houston	David W. Owens
Trey Allen	Cheryl Daniels Howell	LaToya B. Powell
Gregory S. Allison	Jeffrey A. Hughes	William C. Rivenbark
David N. Ammons	Willow S. Jacobson	Dale J. Roenigk
Ann M. Anderson	Robert P. Joyce	John Rubin
Maureen Berner	Diane M. Juffras	Jessica Smith
Mark F. Botts	Dona G. Lewandowski	Meredith Smith
Peg Carlson	Adam Lovelady	Carl W. Stenberg III
Michael Crowell	James M. Markham	John B. Stephens
Leisha DeHart-Davis	Christopher B. McLaughlin	Charles Szypszak
Shea Riggsbee Denning	Kara A. Millonzi	Shannon H. Tufts
Sara DePasquale	Jill D. Moore	Vaughn Mamlin Upshaw
James C. Drennan	Jonathan Q. Morgan	Aimee N. Wall
Richard D. Ducker	Ricardo S. Morse	Jeffrey B. Welty
Joseph S. Ferrell	C. Tyler Mulligan	Richard B. Whisnant
Alyson A. Grine	Kimberly L. Nelson	

Printed in the United States of America

19 18 17 16 15   1 2 3 4 5

ISBN 978-1-56011-847-3

♾ This publication is printed on permanent, acid-free paper in compliance with the North Carolina General Statutes.

♻ Printed on recycled paper

Contents

Chapter 3

Adult Protective Services   35

Chapter 4

Child Protective Services   55

Chapter 5

Health Information   97

Chapter 6

Appendix

Preface

Confidentiality laws are confusing. There are probably too many of them. They overlap, intersect, contradict, and duplicate. At the School of Government, I have the privilege of working with state and county social services officials who are doing critical and difficult work in their communities protecting children and vulnerable adults. They often contact me and my colleagues with questions about confidentiality: May I disclose information in this particular situation? To this particular person? For this particular purpose?

I've studied these laws for years, yet rarely am I able to answer these questions immediately. I usually need to go back to each of the applicable laws and apply them to the facts presented. Sometimes there is a definitive answer to the question. Many times, however, the answer is "it depends" or "maybe." While that is unsatisfying to hear, it is simply the state of the law.

My goal in writing this book and compiling a database of social services confidentiality laws was not to answer all of these questions in black and white. Instead, my goal was simply to make it easier for the social services attorneys and staff to find the answers to the disclosure questions they confront every day.

I want to thank my former School of Government colleagues John Saxon and Janet Mason for paving the way on this challenging topic. Several of my current colleagues wade through the quagmire of confidentiality law with me on a daily basis, and I am so grateful to be able to share ideas—both good and bad—with Mark Botts, Sara DePasquale, and Jill Moore as we work together to answer questions and craft solutions.

This work, particularly the Social Services Confidentiality Law database, would not have been possible without the assistance of Jeffrey Austin. I thank him for his thorough research and extraordinary attention to detail. Angie Stephenson and Rajeev Premakumar with the North Carolina Department of Justice and Nancy Warren with the North Carolina Division of Aging and Adult Services were also extremely helpful with reviewing drafts and providing feedback. Finally, and most importantly, I want to thank my husband and children for their patience and support as I completed this project.

Aimee N. Wall
Thomas Willis Lambeth Distinguished Chair
   in Public Policy
School of Government
The University of North Carolina at Chapel Hill
November 2015

Chapter 1

Introduction

A North Carolina law governing child protective services information provides that "all information received by the department of social services . . . shall be held in *strictest confidence*."[1] Numerous other federal and state laws establish confidentiality protections for protective services information received, created, and maintained by county agencies providing social services.[2] There is also a constitutionally recognized right to informational privacy.[3]

---

1. N.C. GEN. STAT. (hereinafter G.S.) § 7B-302(a1).

2. *See, e.g.*, Administration for Children and Families, *Confidentiality Toolkit: A Resource Tool from the ACF Interoperability Initiative* (Aug. 2014), www.acf.hhs.gov/sites/default/files/assets/acf_confidentiality_toolkit_final_08_12_2014.pdf (a 130-page document discussing federal laws that impact information sharing in social services programs).

3. *See* Whalen v. Roe, 429 U.S. 589, 599–604 (1977) (discussing the basis for a federal constitutional right to information privacy in the context of the government collection of sensitive information); ACT-UP Triangle v. Comm'n for Health Servs., 345 N.C. 699 (1997) (recognizing a state constitutional right to informational privacy).

The confidentiality protection established by this body of law is not absolute.[4] Many state and federal laws allow a county department of social services (DSS) to share information within the department and with other individuals and entities.[5] In fact, information sharing can be an important part of providing social services to an individual or family. Consider the following scenarios:

- A law enforcement officer asks for information about a pending child protective services case. The record includes health information about the child and the child's parents.
- A social worker is trying to contact a disabled adult who is the subject of an adult protective services report. The social worker learns from a neighbor that the disabled adult's son arrived the night before and moved the adult to another state.
- A woman identifies herself as the daughter of a man who is the subject of an adult protective services investigation. She asks for copies of all of the records related to the investigation.
- An eighteen-year-old man explains that he was the subject of a child protective services assessment when he was five years old. He asks for copies of all of the information related to his case.

---

4. *See* Suanna J. Wilson, Confidentiality in Social Work: Issues and Principles 3–4 (1978) (comparing the concepts of absolute and relative confidentiality); Phillip A. Swain, *A Camel's Nose Under the Tent? Some Australian Perspectives on Confidentiality and Social Work Practice*, 36 British Journal of Social Work 91, 105 (2006) ("Why not admit that confidentiality within social work practice is at best a very limited commitment, necessarily constrained by legal impositions, and by accountabilities to agency, bureaucratic and government imperatives?").

5. Former School of Government faculty member John Saxon did extensive research and writing about privacy and confidentiality in the context of social services. That research provides invaluable context for understanding the legal framework for confidentiality law in North Carolina. John L. Saxon, *Confidentiality and Social Services (Part I): What Is Confidentiality?* Social Services Law Bulletin No. 30, Feb. 2001; *Confidentiality and Social Services (Part II): Where Do Confidentiality Rules Come From?* Social Services Law Bulletin No. 31, May 2001; *Confidentiality and Social Services (Part III): A Process for Analyzing Issues Involving Confidentiality*, Social Services Law Bulletin No. 35, Apr. 2002; *Confidentiality and Social Services (Part IV): An Annotated Index of Federal and State Confidentiality Laws*, Social Services Law Bulletin No. 37, Oct. 2002; *Confidentiality and Social Services (Part VI): Collection, Use, and Disclosure of Social Security Numbers*, Social Services Law Bulletin No. 40, Nov. 2005.

- A child who was the subject of a child protective services assessment recently died. A reporter asks DSS for information about the protective services report and assessment.

In all of these situations, DSS staff members will evaluate the request and decide whether information the agency maintains may be disclosed. Former School of Government faculty member John Saxon developed a helpful framework for analyzing these types of confidentiality questions. He suggests using a three-step process for this analysis: (1) define the problem, question, or issue; (2) identify the applicable law or laws; and (3) apply the law or laws to the problem, question, or issue. A more detailed discussion of this framework is included in the Appendix.

The laws that DSS will need to identify and consider vary tremendously. The agency will need to analyze each one to determine the following:

- What type of information does the law apply to?
- Whom does the law apply to?
- When does the law allow information to be disclosed? To whom? And for what purpose?

In the scenarios described above, there may be a strong policy reason for DSS to disclose information. For example, DSS may want to ensure that law enforcement officials have enough information to pursue criminal investigations of abuse, or it may want to preserve and promote the right of individuals to have access to information about themselves. One scholar explains that social workers "define and balance our obligation to safeguard confidential client information with the rights of the individual, organization, and community to access that information."[6]

Consistent with these principles, the applicable laws often try to strike the right balance between protecting an individual's privacy and supporting other interests or policy objectives. There are, however, many laws that are simultaneously trying to accomplish this goal, and they are not always consistent or clear. As a result, county social services officials and attorneys

---

6. Kathleen Millstein, *Confidentiality in Direct Social-Work Practice: Inevitable Challenges and Ethical Dilemmas*, 81 FAMILIES IN SOCIETY 270, 270 (2000). *See also* National Association of Social Workers, *Code of Ethics*, Ethical Standard 1.07(c) (1996) (as amended 2008), www.socialworkers.org/pubs/code/code.asp (explaining that "the general expectation that social workers will keep information confidential does not apply when disclosure is necessary to prevent serious, foreseeable, and imminent harm to a client or other identifiable person."

are often faced with the difficult task of finding the applicable laws and determining how best to apply them in any given situation.

This book is intended to help social services officials with that process by identifying, describing, and analyzing many of the key federal and state confidentiality laws that apply to disclosure of protective services information by county departments of social services. It begins with an overview of the most general, overarching state law that applies to protective services records, Section 108A-80 of the North Carolina General Statutes (hereinafter G.S.) and the accompanying state regulations. The next two chapters explore laws that apply specifically to adult protective services and child protective services, respectively. The following chapter focuses exclusively on disclosure of health-related information, and the final chapter examines the right of individuals to access information about themselves that is contained in a protective services record.

As a companion to this book, the UNC School of Government website (www.sog.unc.edu/resources/tools/social-services-confidentiality-law-index) hosts a searchable database that collects and summarizes many of the applicable state and federal laws that impact confidentiality of social services information.

Before delving into the specific laws, there are a couple of terms that must be defined and some foundational legal concepts that require explanation:

1. What is a "county department of social services"?
2. What is a "disclosure"?
3. How do protective services confidentiality laws intersect with the state's public records laws?
4. What will happen if DSS discloses information in violation of a state or federal confidentiality law?

Each of these questions is discussed in detail below.

What Is a "County Department of Social Services"?

North Carolina operates what is commonly referred to as a "state-supervised, county-administered" social services system.[7] In this type of system,

7. North Carolina General Assembly, Program Evaluation Division, *Statutory Changes Will Promote County Flexibility in Social Services Administration* (May 2011),

counties are required to administer and partially fund certain social services and public assistance programs, including adult and child protective services programs.[8] In most counties, a county department of social services is responsible for administering these programs. Some counties have, instead, created consolidated human services agencies that are responsible for administering these programs.[9] This book will use the phrases "county department of social services" or "county DSS" or the acronym "DSS" to refer to both types of agencies. In short, these terms are intended to encompass any county agency or unit that is responsible for administering social services and public assistance programs.[10]

In some counties, attorneys who are involved with protective services cases are employed by the county DSS. In other counties, the attorneys who do protective services work are employed by the office of the county attorney or by a private law firm. Because records and information received, generated, and maintained by an attorney are subject to another complex body of law, this book does not specifically address disclosure of the attorney's records and information.

---

www.ncleg.net/PED/Reports/2011/DSS.html (describing North Carolina's system of social services administration and comparing it to other state systems).

8. *See* Aimee N. Wall, *Social Services, in* COUNTY AND MUNICIPAL GOVERNMENT IN NORTH CAROLINA 678–81 (Frayda S. Bluestein ed., UNC School of Government 2015); JOHN L. SAXON, SOCIAL SERVICES IN NORTH CAROLINA 32–35 (UNC School of Government, 2008). *See., e.g.*, G.S. 7B-302 (imposing duties on the county director of social services related to child protective services); G.S. 108A-103 (imposing duties on the county director of social services related to adult protective services). *See also* G.S. 108A-74 (authorizing the North Carolina Department of Health and Human Services (NC DHHS) to intervene in the delivery of child protective services and other social services if the county fails to meet its obligations); G.S. 108A-25 (creating public assistance programs and requiring counties or the NC Department of Health and Human Services to administer them).

9. A board of county commissioners is allowed to combine two or more agencies to create a consolidated human services agency. G.S. 153A-77. A consolidated agency may include social services, but it is not required to do so. As of July 2015, twenty-one counties provided social services through a consolidated human services agency. *See* UNC School of Government, Map of NC Public Health & Social Services Agencies (May 1, 2015), www.sog.unc.edu/node/31296.

10. The acronym "DSS" is used elsewhere to refer to the Division of Social Services in the North Carolina Department of Health and Human Services (NC DHHS). This book will use the full name for the division or refer to NC DHHS when addressing issues related to the state agency.

What Is a "Disclosure"?

As discussed above, the scope of this book is relatively narrow. It focuses on the authority of a county department of social services, or DSS, to *disclose* information related to a protective services case. This book will use the terms "disclose" and "disclosure" to mean releasing the information outside the protective services program that created, collected, or maintains it. The following are all examples of disclosures:

- Sharing information with other programs administered by DSS, such as a public assistance program
- Sharing information with public health programs that are part of the same consolidated human services agency as DSS
- Providing information to a law enforcement official, a public agency, a private service provider, a party in a court proceeding, or the court
- Releasing information to the person who is the subject of the information

In order to keep the scope manageable, this book does not address the related concept of "use" of information within a protective services program. For example, it does not explore internal policies that govern how and when a social worker or other staff member involved with a protective services case may access and use information contained in the protective services record.

How Do Protective Services Confidentiality Laws Intersect with the State's Public Records Laws?

Under North Carolina law, many records created by government agencies in the course of conducting the business of government are "public records" and must be made available to members of the public.[11] There are, however, some laws that create exceptions to this requirement. In other words, another law may either *prohibit* disclosure of a public record or *allow* an agency or official to withhold a requested public record.[12]

---

11. *See generally* DAVID LAWRENCE, PUBLIC RECORDS LAW FOR NORTH CARO-LINA LOCAL GOVERNMENTS 4–5 (UNC School of Government, 2d ed. 2009).

12. *See* Frayda Bluestein, *Is This a Public Record? A Framework for Answering Questions About Public Records Requests,* COATES' CANONS: NC LOCAL

While the body of confidentiality law governing protective services information is complex, one concept is relatively simple: DSS is prohibited from disclosing identifiable protective services records in response to a public records request. This prohibition comes primarily from G.S. 108A-80, which makes it unlawful for DSS to disclose identifiable social services information except in limited circumstances. Other laws that make information confidential are also relevant, but this overarching statutory prohibition is an easy starting point.

Some records maintained by DSS related to protective services work will be public records. For example, statistical reports and other de-identified records that the agency generates from protective services records should be treated as public records. However, G.S. 108A-80 specifically protects records "*concerning persons* applying for or receiving public assistance or social services that may be directly or indirectly derived from the records" of DSS.[13] A statistical report that does not identify a person arguably is not a record "concerning" a person, even though it was generated with information about individuals.

What Will Happen If DSS Discloses Information in Violation of a State or Federal Confidentiality Law?

If there is a breach or a violation of a confidentiality law, DSS should take immediate action to investigate the situation. As part of its internal review, the agency will want to determine whether DSS employees should be subject to any personnel action[14] and whether any internal policies or practices should be revised. DSS may want to take steps to mitigate any potential harm that could result from the disclosure. For example, it may be appropriate for DSS to attempt to recover information that was inappropriately disclosed. In addition, DSS may need to notify the client of the disclosure.[15]

GOVERNMENT LAW BLOG (June 9, 2010), http://canons.sog.unc.edu/?p=2592 (discussing exceptions generally).

13. G.S. 108A-80(a) (emphasis added).

14. 10A NCAC 69 .0205 (providing that DSS employees are subject to suspension, dismissal, or disciplinary action for failing to comply with some of the state's confidentiality regulations).

15. 10A NCAC 69 .0506 (requiring DSS to inform the client "to the extent possible" when the agency has released information without the client's consent and

The agency should carefully document the disclosure, as well as the agency's investigation and follow-up.

There may be other consequences that could stem from an inappropriate disclosure, which will vary depending on the law that is violated. For example:

- G.S. 108A-80 provides for criminal penalties.[16]
- The federal substance abuse confidentiality regulations provide for criminal penalties.[17]
- The state communicable disease confidentiality law provides for criminal penalties[18] and civil remedies, such as an injunction.[19]
- The HIPAA privacy regulations include detailed requirements for responding to breaches[20] and provide for both criminal and civil penalties.[21]
- State consumer protection laws also include requirements for responding to security breaches[22] and provide for both criminal and civil penalties, as well as a private right of action.[23]

---

to document the notification). See Chapter 2 for further discussion of this requirement. *See also* G.S. 75-65 (requiring businesses to notify individuals of security breaches in some circumstances); G.S. 132-1.10(c1) (extending the application of the security breach provisions in G.S. 75-65 to government agencies and their employees); Aimee N. Wall, *Health Information Breaches: How Should Health Departments Respond*, COATES' CANONS: NC LOCAL GOVERNMENT LAW BLOG (May 24, 2010), http://canons.sog.unc.edu/?p=2475 (summarizing the state consumer protection law governing security breaches).

16. G.S. 108A-80. There is some ambiguity about the application of the criminal penalties. See the discussion in Chapter 2.

17. 42 C.F.R. § 2.4.

18. G.S. 130A-25 (misdemeanor).

19. G.S. 130A-18.

20. 45 C.F.R. §§ 164.400-414.

21. 42 U.S.C. § 1320d-5 (civil penalties); 42 U.S.C. § 1320d-6 (criminal penalties); 42 C.F.R. § 160.

22. G.S. 75-65 (requiring businesses to notify individuals of security breaches in some circumstances); G.S. 132-1.10(c1) (extending the application of the security breach provisions in G.S. 75-65 to government agencies and their employees).

23. G.S. 75-13 (authorizing criminal enforcement of Chapter 75); G.S. 75-14 (authorizing injunctive relief for violations of Chapter 75); G.S. 75-15.2 (authorizing civil money penalties for violations of G.S. 75-1.1); G.S. 75-65(i) (providing that failure to comply with the security breach requirements is a violation of G.S. 75-1);

Perhaps the most significant consequence in the child protective services arena is the potential for withdrawal of federal or state funding for violations of applicable laws.[24] It is also possible that a person could bring a private lawsuit against the county, the agency, the director, or a DSS employee alleging that his or her constitutional right to privacy was violated[25] or arguing that a disclosure caused emotional distress.[26] While both of these potential consequences—withdrawal of funding and private claims for damages—are conceivable, they appear to be uncommon.

The legal consequences described above are real and can be significant, but DSS will most likely be motivated to avoid violations of applicable laws by the desire to protect individuals and support families. As one researcher noted, "most social workers . . . continue to believe that confidentiality is important for a helping relationship."[27]

G.S. 75-16 (authorizing a private right of action for harm caused by violations of G.S. Chapter 75).

24. G.S. 108A-74 (authorizing NC DHHS to intervene if a county DSS is not providing child protective services, which may include withholding funding).

25. *See* 42 U.S.C. § 1983; ACT-UP Triangle v. Comm'n for Health Servs., 345 N.C. 699 (1997) (recognizing a state constitutional right to informational privacy).

26. *See* Hall v. Post, 323 N.C. 259, 268 (1989) (recognizing a cause of action for intentional inflection of emotional distress based on the unreasonable public disclosure of personal information by a newspaper); Acosta v. Byrum, 180 NC App 562, 568–70 (2006) (recognizing a claim for negligent infliction of emotional distress based on a physician's failure to comply with applicable confidentiality laws); Johnson v. Ruark Obstetrics & Gynecology Assocs., 327 N.C. 283, 304 (1990) (same).

27. MILLSTEIN, *supra* note 6, at 278.

Chapter 2

G.S. 108A-80: The Starting Point

As discussed in Chapter 1, the duty to keep social services information confidential comes from many different sources of law. It is often difficult to know where to start when considering whether to release or share identifiable information. For North Carolina county departments of social services, perhaps the best place to start is with Section 108A-80 of the North Carolina General Statutes (hereinafter G.S.), the one overarching state confidentiality statute that applies to both public assistance programs, such as Medicaid and Work First, and social services, including both child and adult protective services.[1]

After reviewing this state law and the accompanying state regulations,[2] a county department of social services (DSS) can then turn to other laws that may affect the specific type of information involved.

This chapter will help establish the starting point for a confidentiality analysis by addressing the following ten questions:

1. What information is protected by G.S. 108A-80?
2. Who is required to comply with G.S. 108A-80?
3. What does G.S. 108A-80 require, and how does it protect the information?
4. What do the confidentiality regulations that accompany G.S. 108A-80 require?
5. When is DSS required to obtain authorization to disclose confidential information?
6. Is there an authorization form DSS should use?
7. Who is allowed to authorize the disclosure of confidential information?

---

1. The terms "public assistance" and "social services" are not defined in statute. However, the meaning of those terms may be inferred from the overall statutory scheme that governs county departments of social services. For example, N.C. GEN. STAT. (hereinafter G.S.) Chapter 108A, Article 2, creates the programs of public assistance administered by departments of social services (DSS), and the rest of the chapter, together with Chapter 7B, parts of Chapter 110, and parts of other chapters, identifies the department's role and responsibilities with respect to child protective services, child support, foster care, adoption, adult protective services, and other social services programs.

2. The primary body of regulations implementing G.S. 108A-80 is found in Title 10A, Chapter 69, of the North Carolina Administrative Code (hereinafter NCAC).

8. When may DSS disclose confidential information without authorization?
9. Must DSS notify the client if it discloses confidential information without authorization?
10. Must DSS keep a record of disclosures?

The next two chapters will discuss confidentiality laws that are specific to adult protective services and to child protective services, respectively. Each chapter will examine how those laws can be interpreted and applied together with G.S. 108A-80 and the accompanying regulations.

What Information Is Protected by G.S. 108A-80?

G.S. 108A-80 applies to information concerning any person who is applying for or receiving either public assistance or social services if

- the information "may be directly or indirectly derived from the records, files or communications" of the North Carolina Department of Health and Human Services (NC DHHS) or the county board or department of social services, or
- the information "was acquired in the course of performing official duties." [3]

This broad language suggests that the statute applies to information in any form or format: paper, electronic, or oral.

Who Is Required to Comply with G.S. 108A-80?

As drafted, this statute is expansive in scope. It prohibits *any person* from obtaining, disclosing, using, or authorizing, permitting, or acquiescing in the use of the information described above. In practice, however, the statute should be interpreted to apply more narrowly to government officials involved with the administration of public assistance and social services programs. For example, many protective services proceedings are held in open

----

3. G.S. 108A-80(a).

court,[4] and journalists and others are allowed to attend those proceedings and disclose information gathered during them.[5] Those individuals would probably not be required to keep information confidential pursuant to G.S. 108A-80.

If a person who is required to comply with G.S. 108A-80 inappropriately discloses confidential information, he or she may be charged with a Class 1 misdemeanor.[6]

---

4. G.S. 7B-801 (authorizing the judge to close the courtroom for hearings in child protective services cases); *see also* Michael Crowell, *Closing Court Proceedings in North Carolina* (Nov. 2012), www.sog.unc.edu/sites/www.sog.unc.edu/files/Closing%20court%20proceedings%20Nov%2012.pdf.

5. *See* G.S. 7A-276.1 (barring court orders prohibiting publication or broadcast of reports of open court proceedings or reports of public records); Michael Crowell, *Limiting Comments On And Reporting About North Carolina Court Proceedings* (Nov. 2012), www.sog.unc.edu/sites/www.sog.unc.edu/files/Restricting%20reporting%20of%20cases%20Nov%2012.pdf; Janet Mason, *Confidentiality in Juvenile Delinquency Proceedings* Juvenile Law Bulletin No. 2011/01 (May 2011), at 24–26, www.sogpubs.unc.edu/electronicversions/pdfs/jvlb1101.pdf (explaining that the restrictions on disclosing a juvenile's identity in connection with a delinquency case may apply only to those with official duties related to the case and not to the general public or media).

There are, however, rules of practice that place some limitations on the use of cameras in courtrooms in certain types of proceedings (including juvenile, adoption, and child custody proceedings) and for certain types of witnesses (including minors and victims of sex crimes). Gen. R. Pract. Super. & Dist. Cts. 15, 2015 Ann. R. N.C. 12.

6. G.S. 108A-80(b) and (c). G.S. 108A-80 is divided into five subsections. Subsection (a) includes the general requirement that information be kept confidential but does not include any reference to a criminal penalty. Subsections (b) and (c) include specific requirements related to public assistance programs and use of information for political purposes. These two subsections include the following language: "Any violation of this section shall be punishable as a Class 1 misdemeanor." One could argue, therefore, that the general prohibition in subsection (a) does not have a criminal penalty attached. The counterargument is that the plain language of the statute uses the term "section" and not "paragraph" or "subsection" as is the legislative drafting convention. Note that subsection (b1), which was added to G.S. 108A-80 recently, authorizes information sharing with schools and also does not include a specific reference to a criminal penalty.

What Does G.S. 108A-80 Require, and How Does It Protect the Information?

If information is subject to G.S. 108A-80, the general rule is that DSS must obtain authorization to disclose information unless disclosure without authorization is specifically allowed by law. The statute provides that information may be disclosed without authorization for the following limited purposes:

- *Program administration.* Information may be disclosed for purposes directly connected with the administration of the programs of public assistance and social services, in accordance with federal law and state regulations.[7] This general "administration of programs" concept may seem simple and straightforward, but the details are fleshed out in much greater detail in the state regulations (discussed below). In addition, there are program-specific federal and state laws for many of the public assistance and social services programs that must be studied in order to fully understand what types of uses and disclosures are required and permitted.

- *Educational services.* The statute was recently amended to authorize the North Carolina Department of Health and Human Services to share information with schools or the North Carolina Department of Public Instruction as necessary to "establish, coordinate, or maintain appropriate educational services for the person receiving public assistance or social services."[8]

- *Check register access.* G.S. 108A-80 requires the county to provide the public with access to the "recipient check register," which is simply a list of all recipients of assistance from two public assistance programs, Work First and State–County Special Assistance.[9]

The statute also includes an explicit prohibition on the use of any official list of people receiving public assistance or social services as a mailing list for political purposes.[10] The statute does not, however, stand alone. It must be read and applied together with the accompanying state regulations, which are much more detailed and comprehensive.

---

7. G.S. 108A-80(a).

8. G.S. 108A-80(b1) (as amended by S.L. 2014-100, sec. 8.39(a)). See the discussion of disclosure for education-related purposes below.

9. G.S. 108A-80(b). The register is compiled by the North Carolina Department of Health and Human Services and made available to the county finance office.

10. G.S. 108A-80(c).

What Do the Confidentiality Regulations That Accompany G.S. 108A-80 Require?

G.S. 108A-80 authorizes the state's Social Services Commission to adopt regulations (also referred to as rules) governing confidentiality.[11] The regulations, found in the North Carolina Administrative Code, include several sections that address the following concepts related to information sharing and confidentiality:

- *Safeguarding client information.* This section addresses issues such as ownership of records, security and access control, and training for personnel.
- *Clients' access to records.* This section addresses the client's right of access to information about himself or herself. See Chapter 6 for a detailed discussion of the right of access.
- *Sharing information with service providers.* This section focuses on situations where the government agency (DSS or NC DHHS) is purchasing services from another entity or person and needs to share identifiable information with that provider.
- *Disclosing information.* These sections address disclosing information both with and without written authorization from the client or the client's legal representative.

The rest of this chapter will focus on the last section listed above: the provisions that allow DSS to disclose information both with and without permission.[12]

---

11. G.S. 108A-80(d). The Social Services Commission is an administrative body whose primary responsibilities are rulemaking and appointing some members of the county boards of social services. G.S. 143B-153. The commission has thirteen members appointed by the governor, one from each congressional district. G.S. 143-154.

12. The Chapter 69 regulations use the term "consent" to refer to the permission of the individual or the individual's legal representative. Some other confidentiality laws use the term "authorization." *See, e.g.,* 45 C.F.R. 164.508 (HIPAA privacy regulation). The term "consent" is also often used to refer to an individual (or the individual's legal representative) granting a person or entity permission to provide certain services. To minimize confusion, this book will use the term "authorization" throughout to refer to an individual's permission to disclose confidential information.

When Is DSS Required to Obtain Authorization to Disclose Confidential Information?

As discussed earlier, the general rule is that DSS must obtain authorization to disclose information unless disclosure without authorization is specifically allowed by law.[13] This general rule should serve as the starting point for any analysis of whether and with whom confidential DSS records or information may be shared.

Beyond this general rule, there are regulations that specifically *require* authorization in two situations:

- when disclosure is necessary to verify eligibility for assistance or services,[14] and
- when information is being disclosed to a service provider that is under contract with DSS.[15]

While the first provision is self-explanatory, the second provision requires some additional clarification.

Occasionally, DSS contracts with a private or public agency or individual to provide certain services, such as transportation services.[16] Even though these "service providers" are providing services on behalf of DSS, the regulations require that DSS obtain authorization before sharing confidential information with these providers. According to the regulation, the agency may share information with the provider, with the client's authorization, only to the extent necessary to

- determine the service requirements,
- meet the needs of the client, and
- provide eligibility information for reporting purposes.

---

13. G.S. 108A-80; 10A NCAC 69 .0401(c).

14. 10A NCAC 69 .0401. If the person is applying for Work First assistance or State–County Special Assistance, the person must be told about the "recipient check register" described above.

15. 10A NCAC 69 .0601(b).

16. The term "service provider" is defined to mean "any public or private agency or individual from whom the agency purchases services, or authorizes the provision of services provided or purchased by other divisions of the Department of Human Resources." 10A NCAC 69 .0101(7). This regulation was adopted in 1981 and therefore includes an outdated reference to the "Department of Human Resources." An updated version will likely refer to the Department of Health and Human Services.

Despite this restrictive language, an individual could most likely authorize provision of more extensive information to the service provider as long as the authorization was informed (see the discussion of informed authorization below).

A service provider is required to protect the confidentiality of information received in connection with a contract. DSS is required to develop and disseminate policies related to confidential information.[17] In addition, the contract must include language that restricts the provider's use and disclosure of information to "purposes directly connected with the administration of the service program,"[18] and the provider must "protect and preserve" the information as required by the contract.[19]

Interestingly, the regulations also state that any information DSS shares with a service provider is "protected from re-disclosure."[20] While that appears to be a high level of protection for the information, it may not be practical. It is conceivable that DSS and the service provider could agree to some types of re-disclosure not otherwise anticipated by the regulations. For example, a service provider could request permission in the contract to share information with a subcontractor involved with providing a service or performing quality improvement activities. While it seems reasonable that DSS could allow these types of re-disclosures in the contract, it would be prudent to reference this regulation specifically in the contract and include language that prevents inappropriate downstream misuse or re-disclosure.

Is There an Authorization Form DSS May Use?

The North Carolina Department of Health and Human Services provides forms that DSS may use to obtain authorization.[21] Because North Carolina's social services system is state supervised and county administered, it is appropriate for county agencies to use these state-provided forms when seeking authorization.

---

17. 10A NCAC 69 .0603.

18. 10A NCAC 69 .0602.

19. 10A NCAC 69 .0604(a). Failure to comply with the restrictions on use and disclosure may constitute breach of contract. 10A NCAC 69 .0605.

20. 10A NCAC 69 .0604(b).

21. Forms are available online at http://info.dhhs.state.nc.us/olm/forms/.

In order for an authorization to be valid, a state regulation specifically requires that it be informed.[22] DSS must ensure that the individual being asked to sign the form is told

- what information is to be released,
- that there is a definite need for the information,
- that authorization is voluntary and the person may refuse to sign the form,[23] and
- that there are laws that protect the confidentiality of the information.

The state-provided forms include some of this information, but the regulation requires that the individual be "told." Therefore, DSS staff should discuss the form and these specific issues directly with the individual before the form is signed.

Who Is Allowed to Authorize the Disclosure of Confidential Information?

State law identifies three categories of people who may authorize disclosure of information that is protected by G.S. 108A-80:

- the client,
- the client's legal guardian if the client has been adjudicated incompetent, or
- the county department of social services if the client is a minor and in DSS custody.[24]

The last two categories are straightforward and easy to apply. The first is a bit more complicated because the state regulations include a rather expansive definition of the term "client." The term includes

- any applicant for, or recipient of, public assistance;
- any applicant for, or recipient of, social services; and

---

22. 10A NCAC 69 .0404.

23. If an individual is applying for services or assistance and the authorization is requested in order to disclose information to verify eligibility for those services or assistance, DSS may presumably refuse to process the application without the individual's signed authorization.

24. 10A NCAC 69 .0403.

- someone who makes inquiries, is interviewed, or is or has been otherwise served to some extent by the agency.

The term also captures "someone acting responsibly" for the person who has been served by the agency "in accordance with agency policy." This concept likely encompasses a minor's legal guardian or custodian, a parent who has not had his or her parental rights terminated, and, possibly, an attorney. It could also conceivably capture others, such as a person acting *in loco parentis*.[25] State policy manuals do not further define or explain who qualifies as someone acting responsibly, so the term is likely interpreted and applied on a county-by-county basis and may even vary from program to program. See Chapter 6 for a discussion of how the concept of someone acting responsibly for a client may apply in the context of the right of access.

When May DSS Disclose Confidential Information without Authorization?

Staff within DSS are allowed to share confidential information internally as necessary to make referrals, provide supervision and consultation, or determine eligibility for services or programs.[26] DSS is also allowed to disclose information without authorization *outside* the agency in the following situations:

- to the state for purposes of supervision and reporting,
- to other county departments of social services,
- to other governmental entities for purposes of accountability and administration,
- to schools for education-related purposes,
- pursuant to a court order,
- to researchers, and
- in order to comply with other state and federal laws.

---

25. "[T]he term 'in loco parentis' means in the place of a parent, and a 'person in loco parentis' may be defined as one who has assumed the status and obligations of a parent without a formal adoption." *In re* A.P., 165 N.C. App. 841, 845 (2004) (finding that a paternal step-grandfather was not standing *in loco parentis* and was not a custodian with right to appeal an order suspending visitation and approving adoption).

26. 10A NCAC 69 .0501(b)(1). The regulation refers to this type of internal information sharing as a "disclosure." It could also be considered a "use" because the information remains within the same organization.

Below is a brief overview of the law allowing for each of these types of disclosures.

Disclosure to the State for Purposes of Supervision and Reporting

North Carolina operates what is commonly referred to as a state-supervised, county-administered system of social services.[27] Consistent with this integrated relationship, the regulations allow a county DSS to share confidential client information related to both public assistance and social services with NC DHHS for purposes of supervision and reporting.[28] NC DHHS is also required to keep this information confidential pursuant to G.S. 108A-80 and other applicable laws.

Disclosure to Other County Departments of Social Services

County departments of social services are often required to work together to serve clients and therefore may need to share confidential information between counties. The regulations allow for this type of information sharing in the following circumstances:

- County 1 may share information about a public assistance client with County 2 if the client moves from County 1 to County 2 and requests public assistance;[29]
- County 1 may share information about a social services client with County 2 if County 2 is providing services to a client who is in the custody of County 1;[30] and
- County 1 may share information about a social services client with County 2 if County 2 needs the information to "facilitate the provision of a service" requested by County 1.[31]

There are, undoubtedly, other circumstances that will require counties to share confidential information with one another. In order to do so, however, there must be either authorization by the client or a law that allows the release. For example, if a client receiving adult protective services (APS)

---

27. JOHN L. SAXON, SOCIAL SERVICES IN NORTH CAROLINA 31–35 (UNC School of Government, 2008).
28. 10A NCAC 69 .0501(a)(3) (public assistance) and (b)(3) (social services). It seems reasonable to infer that the state is also allowed to share confidential information with the counties.
29. 10A NCAC 69 .0501(a)(2).
30. 10A NCAC 69 .0501(b)(2).
31. 10A NCAC 69 .0501(b)(3).

moves across counties, County 1 may make an APS referral to County 2, and a state regulation allows County 1 to disclose confidential information to County 2 in that circumstance.[32]

Disclosure to Other Governmental Entities for Purposes of Accountability and Administration

The regulations include a section entitled "Disclosures for Purposes of Accountability." The section allows confidential information to be released without authorization

> to federal, state, or county employees for the purpose of monitoring, auditing, evaluating, or facilitating the administration of *other* state and federal programs, provided that the need for the disclosure of confidential information is justifiable for the purpose and that adequate safeguards are maintained to protect the information from re-disclosure.[33]

By its plain language, this section appears to allow a county DSS to share information with other governmental agencies for accountability purposes related to any government program other than the program that generated the information. It also appears to allow information sharing to "facilitate the administration" of any other state or federal program.

If this section is interpreted broadly, a county DSS would be at liberty to share information with other government programs for virtually any program-related purpose, such as eligibility determination, verification of income, and quality improvement. If it is interpreted more narrowly to apply only to information sharing if it is necessary for the purposes of "accountability" (as the title of the section suggests), a county DSS would need to be more cautious about sharing information with other government programs.

A North Carolina Attorney General's Opinion interprets the regulation, in connection with G.S. 108A-80, to allow law enforcement officers to obtain confidential information from a county DSS when investigating whether a client or anyone in the client's household has fraudulently obtained public assistance or social services.[34] The opinion does, however, require the county

---

32. 10A NCAC 71A .0804.

33. 10A NCAC 69 .0503 (emphasis added).

34. Social Services; Public Assistance; Confidentiality of Records; Fraud Investigations by Law Enforcement Officers, 53 N.C. Op. Att'y Gen. 108 (June 5, 1984).

DSS to evaluate the reasonableness of a law enforcement official's request. It states, in part:

> If the county does not think there is reason to suspect fraud, then sound program administration does not permit—much less require—the county department to assist in or conduct a fraud investigation or provide information to those who are.[35]

The opinion acknowledges that other more specific or stringent federal or state laws may conflict with or alter this interpretation and limit disclosure to law enforcement or others for program accountability. Therefore, it is important for DSS to refer not only to G.S. 108A-80 and the accompanying regulations but also to any program-specific statutes and regulations that may apply. There may also be certain types of information that are subject to more restrictions as well, such as information protected by the Federal Substance Abuse Confidentiality regulations (see Chapter 5).

For information that is not subject to a body of confidentiality law other than G.S. 108A-80 and the accompanying regulations, the authority to release information to other government programs for accountability purposes and program administration may be quite expansive. Before making the disclosure, however, DSS must determine that the need for the disclosure is justifiable for the purpose and that adequate safeguards are maintained to protect the information from re-disclosure. Adequate safeguards could include, for example, continuing applicability of G.S. 108A-80 or other laws that protect the confidentiality of information held by the receiving agency.

Disclosure to Schools for Education-Related Purposes

A recent amendment to G.S. 108A-80 added language that allows, but does not require, NC DHHS to share social services and public assistance information with local school administrative units and with the NC Department of Public Instruction.[36] Disclosure must be limited to only the information necessary to establish, coordinate, or maintain appropriate educational services for the person receiving public assistance or social services.

---

35. *Id.*

36. G.S. 108A-80(b1). This paragraph was added to the statute in 2014 and went into effect July 1, 2014. It was added as part of a larger policy effort focused on amending various statutes in order to ensure that children living in private psychiatric residential treatment facilities would receive appropriate educational services. S.L. 2014-100, sec. 8.39.

While this section of the law applies to NC DHHS, county departments of social services probably maintain some or all of the information that may be needed by the school. Because NC DHHS could request the information from a county and then subsequently disclose it to the school, it seems reasonable to assume that a county DSS, as an agent of the state, could disclose the information to the school directly.

Disclosure Pursuant to a Court Order

DSS may disclose information subject to G.S. 108A-80 pursuant to a court order.[37] The term "court order" is defined in the regulations to include "any oral order from a judge or a written document from a judicial official which directs explicitly the release of client information."[38] Despite the language in the regulations, DSS should not rely on an oral order because another state law requires that orders be reduced to writing, signed by the judge, and filed with the clerk of court.[39]

Note that the regulations require that the order "explicitly" direct the release of client information. DSS should not, therefore, infer this specific type of order from a more general directive to "cooperate" or "share records."

A subpoena issued by an attorney is not a court order. Therefore, DSS should not release confidential information in response to a subpoena alone. Rather, the agency should file a motion to quash the subpoena on the grounds that it requests confidential information and no exception for subpoenas applies. In negotiating a consent order or in the course of the hearing, DSS should ask to have the judge review the records *in camera* before issuing any order requiring disclosure. The review will allow the judge to determine whether the need for disclosure clearly outweighs the interests in keeping the information confidential. If appropriate, DSS may consider asking the court to allow the recipient to examine, but not obtain copies of, the information. DSS also may ask the court to order the recipient to protect the information from re-disclosure.

---

37. 10A NCAC 69 .0505.

38. 10A NCAC 69 .0101. Interestingly, the regulation recognizes oral orders from judges but not from other judicial officials, such as clerks of court.

39. G.S. 1A-1, Rule 58 ("Subject to the provisions of Rule 54(b), a judgment is entered when it is reduced to writing, signed by the judge, and filed with the clerk of court.").

Disclosure to Researchers

The regulations allow DSS to release confidential information without authorization for research purposes.[40] Such requests must be in writing and must include

- an explanation of how the research may expand knowledge and improve professional practices,
- a description of how the study will be conducted and how the findings will be used,
- a presentation of the individual's credentials in the area of investigation,
- a description of how the individual will safeguard the information, and
- an assurance that no report will contain the names of individuals or any other identifiable information.

Note that DSS is not required to disclose information to researchers even when presented with a request that meets all of the above requirements. The county may refuse the request.

It is also important to consider this regulation in the context of other laws that protect the confidentiality of the specific type of information being requested by the researcher. If, for example, the researcher is requesting copies of identifiable child protective services records, state statutes and regulations likely prohibit the disclosure (see Chapter 4). If the information is subject to the federal substance abuse confidentiality regulation or the HIPAA privacy regulation, any disclosure to researchers will be either prohibited or subject to additional restrictions and administrative requirements (see Chapter 5).

Disclosure in Order to Comply with Other Laws

If another state or federal law requires disclosure of confidential information, the state regulations allow the disclosure.[41] Some might argue that this provision is the exception that swallows the rule of confidentiality. Rather than viewing this exception as an overbroad loophole, one could think of

---

40. 10A NCAC 69 .0502.

41. If a disclosure is required by state law but expressly prohibited by federal law, the federal law would prevail. *See* 10A NCAC 69 .0201 ("Whenever there is an inconsistency between federal or state statutes or regulations specifically

it as a reasonable approach to balancing public policy interests in all areas of the law. The regulators recognized that they may not always be able to anticipate circumstances where information would be needed and therefore deferred to the legislative and regulatory processes. If other elected and appointed policymakers conclude that the need for the information in a particular circumstance outweighs the privacy interests involved, the regulations allow the disclosure.

Two examples of laws that DSS may encounter govern (1) disclosures to protection and advocacy systems and (2) access by members of the agency's governing board. Both are discussed below. Other examples specific to adult protective services and child protective services are discussed in Chapters 3 and 4. Note that the examples identified in this book are not exhaustive. Other laws may authorize or require disclosure of confidential information maintained by DSS. The agency will need to work with its attorney to review the law and determine how to interpret that law in the context of the other applicable confidentiality laws.

Disclosure to Protection and Advocacy Systems

Federal law provides that a state-funded protection and advocacy organization, such as Disability Rights North Carolina, must be provided with prompt access to records if it is investigating potential abuse or neglect of a person with a developmental disability or mental illness at a facility that is providing services to that person.[42] The laws apply to records of agencies charged with investigating abuse, neglect, injury, or death of a person at a facility or location that is providing services or care to individuals in this specific population. Because this federal law *requires* disclosure of information, DSS must make the disclosure. State confidentiality laws, including the laws specific to child protective services discussed in Chapter 4, will not override this federal mandate.

---

addressing confidentiality issues, the agency shall abide by the statute or regulation which provides more protection for the client.").

42. 42 U.S.C. 15043 (1975); 42 U.S.C. 10805–10826 (1986). The law does not grant access to records of all individuals with developmental disabilities or mental illness in facilities. It applies if the individual or the individual's legal representative has authorized access or in some situations where the system has received a complaint or has probable cause to believe that the individual has been subject to abuse or neglect. 42 U.S.C. 15043(a)(2)(H); 42 U.S.C. 10805(a)(4).

Access by Members of the Agency's Governing Board

A state statute provides that members of a county board of social services must be allowed to have access to confidential social services and public assistance information upon request.[43] If a county has a consolidated human services board instead of a social services board, this right of access belongs to the members of the consolidated board.[44] If a county's board of commissioners has abolished either the board of social services or the consolidated human services board and assumed the abolished board's powers and duties, this right of access belongs to the members of the board of county commissioners.[45]

Because this is a state law rather than a federal law, DSS will need to carefully consider whether federal or *other* state laws conflict with this law. G.S. 108A-80 and the accompanying regulations are likely not in conflict because disclosure is allowed (1) for purposes of accountability and administration, as discussed above,[46] and (2) as necessary to comply with other laws.[47] See Chapter 4 for a discussion of how this requirement intersects with the child protective services laws.

Must DSS Notify the Client If It Discloses Information without Authorization?

If information is disclosed without authorization, DSS is required to inform the client of the disclosure "to the extent possible" and document the notification in the client's record.[48] If DSS is unable to locate the client to make the notification, the agency is expected to document its attempts to do so.

---

43. G.S. 108A-11.
44. G.S. 153A-77(d) ("Except as otherwise provided, the consolidated human services board shall have the powers and duties conferred by law upon . . . a social services board.").
45. G.S. 153A-77(a).
46. 10A NCAC 69 .0503.
47. 10A NCAC 69 .0504.
48. 10A NCAC 69 .0506. *See also* 45 C.F.R. 205.50(a)(2)(iii) (federal regulation governing confidentiality of some child protective services records requiring the agency to notify an individual or the individual's family if information has been or will be disclosed without permission).

Some similar laws include exceptions to the notice requirement or allow notice to the client to be delayed in some circumstances.[49] For example, a law enforcement official may not want DSS to notify a client right away that the agency disclosed certain information to the law enforcement official because of concerns that doing so could compromise an investigation.

While the regulation requiring DSS to provide notice does not include any specific exceptions, the language "to the extent possible" suggests that there may be some flexibility with this requirement. Similar language is included in the code of ethics adopted by the National Association of Social Workers.[50]

Must DSS Keep a Record of Disclosures?

Yes. If DSS discloses client information, it must document the disclosure in the client's record. If the disclosure was made pursuant to the client's authorization, a copy of the signed form should be included in the record.[51] If the disclosure was made without authorization, the agency must include appropriate documentation in the record, such as a copy of the court order or the researcher's written request. If there is no written record to include, DSS should create one.[52]

---

49. *See, e.g.*, G.S. 108A-117 (requiring notice to a client when a subpoena has been issued directing a financial institution to produce records in a financial exploitation investigation but allowing the notice to be delayed in some circumstances).

50. *See* National Association of Social Workers, *Code of Ethics*, Ethical Standard 1.07(d) (1996) (as amended 2008), www.socialworkers.org/pubs/code/code.asp ("Social workers should inform clients, to the extent possible, about the disclosure of confidential information and the potential consequences, when feasible before the disclosure is made. This applies whether social workers disclose confidential information on the basis of a legal requirement or client consent.").

51. 10A NCAC 69 .0406.

52. 10A NCAC 69 .0507.

Relevant Statute
North Carolina General Statutes

§ 108A-80. Confidentiality of records.

(a) Except as provided in subsections (b) and (b1) of this section, it shall be unlawful for any person to obtain, disclose or use, or to authorize, permit, or acquiesce in the use of any list of names or other information concerning persons applying for or receiving public assistance or social services that may be directly or indirectly derived from the records, files or communications of the Department or the county boards of social services, or county departments of social services or acquired in the course of performing official duties except for the purposes directly connected with the administration of the programs of public assistance and social services in accordance with federal law, rules and regulations, and the rules of the Social Services Commission or the Department.

(b) The Department shall furnish a copy of the recipient check register monthly to each county auditor showing a complete list of all recipients of Work First Family Assistance in Standard Program Counties and State-County Special Assistance, their addresses, and the amounts of the monthly grants. An Electing County whose checks are not being issued by the State shall furnish a copy of the recipient check register monthly to its county auditor showing a complete list of all recipients of Work First Family Assistance in the Electing County, their addresses, and the amounts of the monthly payments. These registers shall be public records open to public inspection during the regular office hours of the county auditor, but the registers or the information contained therein may not be used for any commercial or political purpose. Any violation of this section shall constitute a Class 1 misdemeanor.

(b1) The Department may share confidential information concerning a person receiving public assistance or social services with a local school administrative unit and with the Department of Public Instruction. Disclosure is limited to that information necessary to establish, coordinate, or maintain appropriate educational services for the person receiving public assistance or social services.

(c) Any listing of recipients of benefits under any public assistance or social services program compiled by or used for official purposes by a county board of social services or a county department of social services shall not be used as a mailing list for political purposes. This prohibition shall apply to any list of recipients of benefits of any federal, State, county or mixed public assistance or social services program. Further, this prohibition shall apply to the use of such listing by any person, organization, corporation, or business, including but not limited to public officers or employees of federal, State, county, or other local governments, as a mailing list for political purposes. Any violation of this section shall be punishable as a Class 1 misdemeanor.

(d) The Social Services Commission may adopt rules governing access to case files for social services and public assistance programs, except the Medical Assistance Program. The Secretary of the Department of Health and Human Services shall have the authority to adopt rules governing access to medical assistance case files.

Relevant Regulations
North Carolina Administrative Code
TITLE 10A—HEALTH AND HUMAN SERVICES
CHAPTER 69—CONFIDENTIALITY AND ACCESS TO CLIENT RECORDS

SECTION .0100—GENERAL PROVISIONS

10A NCAC 69 .0101   DEFINITIONS

As used in this Subchapter, unless the context clearly requires otherwise, the following terms have the meanings specified:

(1) "Client" means any applicant for, or recipient of, public assistance or services, or someone who makes inquiries, is interviewed, or is or has been otherwise served to some extent by the agency. For purposes of this Subchapter, someone acting responsibly for the client in accordance with agency policy is subsumed under the definition of client.

(2) "Agency" means the state Division of Social Services and the county departments of social services, unless separately identified.

(3) "Client information" or "client record" means any information, whether recorded or not and including information stored in computer data banks or computer files, relating to a client which was received in connection with the performance of any function of the agency.

(4) "Director" means the head of the state Division of Social Services or the county departments of social services.

(5) "Delegated representative" means anyone designated by the director to carry out the responsibilities established by the rules in this Subchapter. Designation is implied when the assigned duties of an employee require access to confidential information.

(6) "Court order" means any oral order from a judge or a written document from a judicial official which directs explicitly the release of client information.

(7) "Service provider" means any public or private agency or individual from whom the agency purchases services, or authorizes the provision of services provided or purchased by other divisions of the Department of Human Resources.

SECTION .0400—RELEASE OF CLIENT INFORMATION

10A NCAC 69 .0401   PROCEDURE FOR OBTAINING CONSENT FOR RELEASE OF INFORMATION

(a) As a part of the application process for public assistance or services, the client shall be informed of the need for and give consent to the release of information necessary to verify statements to establish eligibility.

(b) As a part of the application process for Aid to Families with Dependent children, and State or County Special Assistance for Adults, the client shall be informed of the requirement for listing of the public assistance recipient's name, address, and amount of the monthly grant in a public record open to public inspection during the regular office hours of the county auditor.

(c) No individual shall release any client information which is owned by the state Division of Social Services or the county departments of social services, or request the release of information regarding the client from other agencies or individuals without obtaining a signed consent for release of information. Disclosure without obtaining consent shall be in accordance with Section .0500 of this Subchapter.

10A NCAC 69 .0402   CONSENT FOR RELEASE OF INFORMATION

(a) The consent for release of information shall be on a form provided by the state Division of Social Services or shall contain the following:

 (1) name of the provider and the recipient of the information;
 (2) the extent of information to be released;
 (3) the name and dated signature of the client;
 (4) a statement that the consent is subject to revocation at any time except to the extent that action has been taken in reliance on the consent;
 (5) length of time the consent is valid.

(b) The client may alter the form to contain other information which may include but is not limited to:

 (1) a statement specifying the date, event or condition upon which the consent may expire even if the client does not expressly revoke the consent;
 (2) specific purpose for the release.

10A NCAC 69 .0403   PERSONS WHO MAY CONSENT TO THE RELEASE OF INFORMATION

The following persons may consent to the release of information:

 (1) the client;
 (2) the legal guardian if the client has been adjudicated incompetent;
 (3) the county department of social services if the client is a minor and in the custody of the county department of social services.

10A NCAC 69 .0404   INFORMED CONSENT

Prior to obtaining a consent for release of information, the delegated representative shall explain the meaning of informed consent. The client shall be told the following:

 (1) contents to be released;
 (2) that there is a definite need for the information;
 (3) that the client can give or withhold the consent and the consent is voluntary;
 (4) that there are statutes and regulations protecting the confidentiality of the information.

10A NCAC 69 .0405   PERSONS DESIGNATED TO RELEASE CLIENT INFORMATION

Directors and their delegated representatives, as defined, may release client information in accordance with rules in Section .0400 of this Subchapter.

10A NCAC 69 .0406   DOCUMENTATION OF RELEASE

Whenever client information is released on the basis of a consent as defined in .0402 of this Subchapter, the director or delegated representative shall place a copy of the signed consent in the appropriate client record.

SECTION .0500—DISCLOSURE OF CLIENT INFORMATION WITHOUT CLIENT CONSENT

10A NCAC 69 .0501   DISCLOSURE WITHIN THE AGENCY

(a) Client information from the public assistance record may be disclosed without the consent of the client under the following circumstances:

    (1)   to other employees of the county department of social services for purposes of making referrals, supervision, consultation or determination of eligibility;

    (2)   to other county departments of social services when the client moves to that county and requests public assistance;

    (3)   between the county departments of social services and the state Division of Social Services for purposes of supervision and reporting.

(b) Client information from the service record may be disclosed without the consent of the client under the following circumstances:

    (1)   to other employees of the county department of social services for purposes of making referrals, supervision, consultation or determination of eligibility;

    (2)   to another county department of social services when that county department of social services is providing services to a client who is in the custody of the county department of social services;

    (3)   to another county department of social services to the extent necessary to facilitate the provision of a service requested by referring county department of social services;

    (4)   between the county department of social services and the state Division of Social Services for purposes of supervision and reporting.

10A NCAC 69 .0502   DISCLOSURE FOR THE PURPOSE OF RESEARCH

Client information may be disclosed without the consent of the client to individuals requesting approval to conduct studies of client records, provided such approval is requested in writing and the written request will specify and be approved on the basis of:

    (1)   an explanation of how the findings of the study have potential for expanding knowledge and improving professional practices;

    (2)   a description of how the study will be conducted and how the findings will be used;

    (3)   a presentation of the individual's credentials in the area of investigation;

    (4)   a description of how the individual will safeguard information;

    (5)   an assurance that no report will contain the names of individuals or any other information that makes individuals identifiable.

10A NCAC 69 .0503   DISCLOSURE FOR PURPOSES OF ACCOUNTABILITY

Client information may be disclosed without the consent of the client to federal, state, or county employees for the purpose of monitoring, auditing, evaluating, or facilitating the administration of other state and federal programs, provided that the need for the disclosure of confidential information is justifiable for the purpose and that adequate safeguards are maintained to protect the information from re-disclosure.

10A NCAC 69 .0504   DISCLOSURE PURSUANT TO OTHER LAWS

Client information may be disclosed without the consent of the client for purposes of complying with other state and federal statutes and regulations.

10A NCAC 69 .0505   DISCLOSURE PURSUANT TO A COURT ORDER

Client information may be disclosed without the consent of the client in response to a court order, as defined.

10A NCAC 69 .0506   NOTICE TO CLIENT

When information is released without the client's consent, the client shall be informed to the extent possible, of the disclosure. The method of informing the client of the disclosure shall be documented in the appropriate record.

10A NCAC 69 .0507   DOCUMENTATION OF DISCLOSURE

Whenever client information is disclosed in accordance with Section .0500 of this Subchapter, the director or delegated representative shall ensure that documentation of the disclosure is placed in the appropriate client record.

10A NCAC 69 .0508   PERSONS DESIGNATED TO DISCLOSE INFORMATION

Directors and their delegated representatives, as defined, may disclose client information in accordance with Section .0500 of this Subchapter.

Chapter 3

Adult Protective Services

Under North Carolina law, the government—through the county department responsible for social services—has a duty to provide protective services to any "disabled adult" who has been abused, neglected, or exploited
financially.[1] A disabled adult is a person who

- is age eighteen or older or is a legally emancipated minor,

---

1. N.C. GEN. STAT. (hereinafter G.S.) §§ 108A-103 to -108.

- is present in the state, and
- is physically or mentally incapacitated.[2]

Any person who suspects that a disabled adult needs services to protect him or her from abuse, neglect, or financial exploitation must submit an oral or written report to the county department of social services (DSS).[3] Upon receiving the report, DSS is required to conduct an evaluation to determine whether the disabled adult is in need of services and, if so, what services are needed. DSS must then take steps to ensure that the services are provided.[4] Needed services will vary from person to person but could include, for example, providing medical care or food, finding adequate shelter, and protecting the person from mistreatment or financial exploitation.

This chapter is designed to answer only one question:

> When may DSS disclose identifiable adult protective services (APS) information without authorization?

The chapter will first provide an overview of the legal landscape in this area. It will then discuss how to interpret and apply the combination of federal and state laws, including G.S. 108A-80, in several key areas related to the administration of APS programs.

---

2. G.S. 108A-101(d). According to the state law, the physical or mental incapacity must be due to "mental retardation, cerebral palsy, epilepsy or autism; organic brain damage caused by advanced age or other physical degeneration in connection therewith; or conditions incurred at any age which are the result of accident, organic brain damage, mental or physical illness, or continued consumption or absorption of substances."

3. G.S. 108A-102. New reporting requirements related to residents in certain facilities go into effect December 1, 2015. *See* Aimee N. Wall, *Adult Protective Services: A New Reporting Requirement*, COATES' CANONS: NC LOCAL GOVERNMENT LAW BLOG (June 23, 2015), canons.sog.unc.edu/?p=8142.

4. A detailed discussion of the adult protective services (APS) law is beyond the scope of this book. *See* G.S. Chapter 108A, Article 6 (general laws governing abuse, neglect, and financial exploitation of disabled adults) and Article 6A (specific laws related to financial exploitation).

Overview of the Legal Landscape

Confidentiality of APS information is governed primarily by state law.[5] The first laws to consider are the overarching state statute, Section 108A-80 of the North Carolina General Statutes (hereinafter G.S.), and the accompanying regulations in Chapter 69 of the North Carolina Administrative Code (hereinafter NCAC). As discussed in Chapter 2, these state laws require DSS to protect client information but allow it to disclose information without authorization in several circumstances, including

- to the state for purposes of supervision and reporting,
- to other county departments of social services,
- to other governmental entities for purposes of accountability and administration,
- to schools for education-related purposes,
- pursuant to a court order,
- to researchers, and
- in order to comply with other state and federal laws.

In addition to G.S. 108A-80 and the NCAC Chapter 69 regulations, there are several state regulations in NCAC Chapter 71A that specifically address confidentiality of APS information.[6] These regulations create heightened protection for certain types of information and expressly allow or require disclosure in certain situations. All of these additional regulations are discussed in more detail below.

---

5. The state and counties receive some federal funding to support APS programs through the Social Services Block Grant. 42 U.S.C. § 1397 *et seq.* This funding does not appear to impose any legal duties on the state or the counties to protect the confidentiality of information collected or maintained by APS programs. The federal Older Americans Act does include a limited reference to confidentiality. 42 U.S.C. § 3027(a)(12)(C). According to staff at the NC Division of Aging and Adult Services, North Carolina does not rely on this funding source for DSS administration of APS programs. Email from Nancy Warren, NC Division of Aging and Adult Services (May 26, 2015) (on file with author). As a result, those confidentiality requirements are not incorporated into the analysis in this chapter. If the federal funding sources for county APS programs change, it is possible that federal confidentiality laws will need to be evaluated and considered as part of the analysis.

6. N.C. Admin. Code (hereinafter NCAC) title 10A, ch. 71A.

Information with Heightened Protection

Identity of the Reporter and Others with Information

As mentioned above, state law requires that all people report to DSS suspected abuse, neglect, or exploitation of a disabled adult. Pursuant to G.S. 108A-80, the identity of the reporter and the information provided by the reporter are confidential and may only be disclosed when authorized or required by law. A state regulation, however, specifically allows DSS to disclose the reporter's identity in three specific situations:[7]

- when a court orders disclosure,[8]
- to the Division of Health Service Regulation[9] when division staff request information to carry out an investigation, and
- to the district attorney's office or law enforcement officials involved with a criminal investigation of alleged abuse, neglect, or exploitation.[10]

The same rules apply to the identity of any other person who provides information to DSS in the course of an investigation.

Because this regulation provides somewhat heightened protection for the identity of the reporter and others with information, it overrides any of the other regulations in Chapter 69 that allow disclosure without authorization, such as the provisions allowing disclosures for research.

Specific Findings

When DSS receives a report of abuse, neglect, or exploitation, it will conduct a comprehensive evaluation of the disabled adult and document its findings. If DSS finds evidence of abuse, neglect, or exploitation, or if the subject of the evaluation was or is a resident of a facility (such as an adult care home), the

---

7. 10A NCAC 71A .0802.

8. This is consistent with the provision in the Chapter 69 regulations authorizing disclosure pursuant to a court order. 10A NCAC 69 .0505. There is no definition of the term "court order" in the Chapter 71A regulations; therefore, it is reasonable to rely on the definition used in the Chapter 69 regulations. *See* 10A NCAC 69 .0101 ("... written document from a judicial official which directs explicitly the release of client information").

9. The Division of Health Service Regulation is responsible for oversight of medical, mental health, and adult care facilities as well as emergency medical services and local jails.

10. 10A NCAC 71A .0802.

agency will prepare a written report of the evaluation, which must include the following:

- the name, address, age, and condition of the adult;
- the allegations (but not the identity of the reporter);
- the evaluation, including the agency's findings, and supporting documents, which include any psychological or medical reports;
- conclusions; and
- recommendations for action.[11]

These records are all confidential under G.S. 108A-80. In addition, a regulation in Chapter 71A appears to provide heightened confidentiality protection for "specific findings" included in the agency's evaluation report.[12] According to these regulations, DSS may disclose findings only in the following circumstances:

- pursuant to the disabled adult's authorization;[13]
- pursuant to a court order;
- to other persons or agencies as necessary to provide protective services;[14]
- to the district attorney or law enforcement agencies upon request, but only if evidence of abuse, neglect, or exploitation is found;[15]
- to federal, state, and law enforcement agencies when the results of the protective services evaluation indicate violations of other laws enforced by those agencies;[16] and

---

11. 10A NCAC 71A .0901(b). The report form provided by the State Division of Aging and Adult Services includes a section entitled "APS Findings and Conclusions." *See Written Report of Adult Protective Services Evaluation* (Aug. 6, 2013), www.ncdhhs.gov/aging/adultsvcs/afs_aps_tool.htm.

12. 10A NCAC 71A .0803.

13. It is not clear whether the authorization of a disabled adult's legal representative (such as a guardian) would be sufficient. Because the Chapter 71A regulations are silent in this regard but the Chapter 69 regulations expressly allow it, one could argue that the legal representative is not allowed to authorize disclosure of this particular category of information. *Compare* 71A NCAC .0803 *with* 10A NCAC 69 .0403.

14. The regulations provide that this type of disclosure is at the discretion of DSS. They also state that this disclosure is expressly allowed without the authorization of the disabled adult or the adult's caretaker.

15. 10A NCAC 71A .0803.

16. 10A NCAC 71A .0806.

- to certain agencies within the North Carolina Department of Health and Human Services (NC DHHS) when DSS has substantiated a report of abuse, neglect, or exploitation.[17]

Because these regulations provide heightened protection for this particular category of information—specific findings—the other disclosures allowed by the Chapter 69 regulations are not permissible.[18] For example, DSS should not disclose specific findings to researchers or governmental entities for the purposes of accountability and administration of programs other than APS.

DSS may still disclose specific findings consistent with the Chapter 69 regulations that allow disclosure pursuant to authorization or a court order and to the state and other counties in the context of providing protective services. Those types of disclosures are also consistent with the Chapter 71A regulations governing specific findings.

The Chapter 69 regulations also allow disclosure when necessary to comply with other laws. While the Chapter 71A regulations do not expressly include that language, it would still be appropriate for DSS to comply with a federal or state statute that requires disclosure.

Financial Records and Reports Received from Financial Institutions

In cases involving financial exploitation of a disabled adult, DSS has the authority to obtain copies of records from financial institutions.[19] Those records are subject to heightened confidentiality protections. The statute provides:

> All produced copies of the disabled adult's or older adult's financial records . . . shall be kept confidential by the investigating entity unless required by court order to be disclosed to a party to a court proceeding or introduced and admitted into evidence in an open court proceeding.[20]

---

17. 10A NCAC 71A .0806.

18. 10A NCAC 69 .0201 ("Whenever there is inconsistency between federal or state statutes or regulations specifically addressing confidentiality issues, the agency shall abide by the statute or regulation which provides more protection for the client.").

19. G.S. Chapter 108A, Article 6A. *See* Aimee N. Wall, *Financial Exploitation of Older Adults and Disabled Adults: An Overview of North Carolina Law*, SOCIAL SERVICES LAW BULLETIN No. 43 (Oct. 2014).

20. G.S. 108A-116(d).

Because of this requirement, DSS should not disclose financial records collected as part of a financial exploitation investigation unless directed to do so by the court.

Interestingly, G.S. 108-116 also extends this heightened confidentiality protection to "any information obtained pursuant to the duty to report found in G.S. 108A-115."[21] The reporting requirement referenced in the law directs financial institutions and their officers and employees to report suspected financial exploitation of a disabled adult to DSS. This requirement is redundant because another, earlier statute already requires such reporting.[22] One could argue, though, that the more specific, later enacted statute affording heightened protection should apply to all information in the report as well as to the financial records obtained whenever DSS receives a report from a financial institution (or its employees or officers).[23] The heightened protection would not apply to the information DSS receives in a report of suspected financial exploitation if it is received from a person who is not connected to the financial institution.

---

21. *Id.*

22. G.S. 108A-102 ("Any person having reasonable cause to believe that a disabled adult is in need of protective services shall report such information to the director."); G.S. 108A-101(n) (defining "protective services" to mean "services provided by the State or other government or private organizations or individuals which are necessary to protect the disabled adult from abuse, neglect, or exploitation."). The other reporting requirement was added to the law in 2013. S.L. 2013-337.

23. The newer reporting requirement in G.S. 108A-115 is more expansive than the older reporting requirement in G.S. 108A-102. It requires reports related to any person sixty-five years of age or older regardless of whether the adult is disabled. Also, it requires reports to be made to law enforcement officials and also to trusted individuals identified by the adult, if any. That more expansive body of information is certainly subject to the heightened confidentiality protection in G.S. 108A-116(d), but because it will not be part of DSS's adult protective services record, it is beyond the scope of this discussion.

Specific Types of Disclosures

Disclosure to Law Enforcement Officials

Providing protective services to adults often requires close collaboration between DSS and law enforcement agencies. State law reflects the importance of this relationship—it includes several specific provisions that either require or allow DSS to share APS information with law enforcement officials.

Mandatory and Discretionary Notification

DSS is required to notify the district attorney if it finds evidence indicating that a disabled adult has been abused, neglected, or exploited.[24] This notification must be in writing and must include the same information that is provided in the written report of evaluation described above. Typically, the reports will not include the identity of the reporter.

There is often heightened concern about the confidentiality of health-related information. Because state law specifically *requires* the disclosure of psychological and medical reports, DSS will be able to disclose that type of information unless the information is subject to the federal substance abuse confidentiality regulations. For further discussion of the disclosure of health information, see Chapter 5.

The mandatory notification requirement discussed above applies after an APS investigation is complete. However, DSS is allowed to contact the district attorney or law enforcement officials immediately after receiving the initial report if there is reason to believe that physical harm to the disabled adult may occur. In this situation, DSS is allowed to share with officials information that would otherwise be confidential, including most health information.[25] The agency may also provide law enforcement officials information from the Adult Protective Services Register "to assure that protective services will be made available to an adult as quickly as possible."[26]

---

24. G.S. 108A-109.

25. DSS would not have the authority to disclose information subject to the federal substance abuse confidentiality law. See the discussion in Chapter 5.

26. 10A NCAC 71A .0806(b)(1)(C).

Responding to a Request

As mentioned above, "specific findings" are subject to heightened protection under the Chapter 71A regulations. If, however, the district attorney or a law enforcement official requests information to help with a criminal investigation or prosecution of abuse, neglect, or exploitation, DSS is required to provide a copy of the specific findings.[27] Presumably, if DSS found evidence of abuse, neglect, or exploitation, it would have already provided the district attorney with a copy of the written report of evaluation, which includes the specific findings. There may, however, be circumstances in which DSS does not provide such a notification or a law enforcement official is seeking information independently for an investigation. In these instances, it is clear that DSS may provide either the district attorney or a law enforcement official with the evaluation upon request.

Identity of the Reporter or Others with Information

As discussed above, the law provides heightened confidentiality protections for the identity of the person who filed a protective services report and the identity of any person who provided information to DSS in the course of its investigation. DSS is allowed to disclose the identities of these individuals to the district attorney or to law enforcement officials if those officials are prosecuting or conducting a criminal investigation related to the alleged abuse, neglect, or exploitation.[28]

Court Order

If a court orders DSS to disclose APS information—including the agency's specific findings—to a district attorney or law enforcement official, DSS must comply with that order.[29] The definition of "court order" is broad and includes "any oral order from a judge or a written document from a judicial official" that explicitly directs the release of client information.[30] This definition includes a search warrant. Because there is clear authority for

---

27. 10A NCAC 71A .0803.

28. 10A NCAC 71A .0802.

29. 10A NCAC 69 .0505 (allowing disclosure pursuant to a court order); 10A NCAC 71A .0803 (allowing disclosure of specific findings in response to a court order).

30. 10A NCAC 69 .0101. See Chapter 2 for a discussion of the need for any such order to be written rather than oral.

DSS to disclose APS information to district attorneys and law enforcement officials upon request in the context of a prosecution or investigation of alleged abuse, neglect, or exploitation, it is unlikely that such officials will need to seek a court order in those cases. There may be other types of criminal investigations, however, that could result in a court order being issued.

Violations of Other Laws

If an APS evaluation reveals information suggesting violations of statutes, rules, or regulations other than the laws governing abuse, neglect, and exploitation of disabled adults, DSS is allowed—but not required—to send a copy of the written report of evaluation to the appropriate federal or state law enforcement agencies.[31] For example, although DSS's authority is limited to abuse, neglect, and exploitation of *disabled* adults, the criminal laws address not only disabled adults but also *older* adults.[32] If DSS concludes that an older adult is not disabled but still may have been abused, neglected, or exploited, it may share a copy of the written report of evaluation with law enforcement officials.

Disclosure to Another County or to the State for the Purpose of Providing Protective Services

As discussed above, there is broad authority to share "specific findings" without the disabled adult's permission with other people or agencies, including agencies in other counties or states, to the extent necessary to provide protective services to the adult.[33] In addition to this broad authority, Chapter 71A includes additional provisions that apply when the adult moves from one county to another. If the adult is receiving court-ordered protective services at the time of the move, the first county must make a referral to the second county.[34] The first county is allowed to share information related to the services and the need for services with the second county without the adult's

---

31. 10A NCAC 71A .0805.

32. G.S. 14-32.3 (domestic abuse or neglect of disabled or elder adults; includes adults over age sixty); G.S. 14-112.2 (financial exploitation of disabled and older adults; includes adults over age sixty-five).

33. The regulations provide that this type of disclosure is at the discretion of DSS. They also state that this disclosure is expressly allowed without the authorization of the disabled adult or the adult's caretaker.

34. 10A NCAC 71A .0702(b).

permission. If the second county asks for information, the first county is required to share it.[35] If the disabled adult is receiving protective services pursuant to his or her own consent at the time of the move, rather than pursuant to a court order, the first county must ask the adult's permission to share information with the second county.[36]

DSS is also allowed to share information from the Adult Protective Services Register with protective services or law enforcement agencies in other states "to assure that protective services will be made available to an adult previously served in North Carolina as quickly as possible . . . ."[37]

Disclosure to Collateral Contacts

When DSS is conducting an evaluation to determine whether protective services are needed, the agency will likely interview people who may have information about the disabled adult's situation. Those people, referred to as "collateral contacts," may be curious about the investigation or ask questions about the adult's situation. The state regulations anticipate these contacts and imply that some very limited information sharing with them is allowed.[38] DSS must be careful not to share too much information because all of the information DSS is acquiring is protected by G.S. 108A-80. The state manual expands on the concept of sharing with collateral contacts by explaining that the county's response to such inquiries "should be in general terms about the agency's concern for the adult and need for information to determine whether or not the agency can provide assistance."[39]

---

35. 10A NCAC 71A .0804.

36. 10A NCAC 71A .0702(a).

37. 10A NCAC 71A .0806(a)(1).

38. 10A NCAC 71A .0801 ("Collateral contacts with persons knowledgeable about a disabled adult's situation may be made without the adult or caretaker's consent when such contacts are necessary to complete a protective services evaluation.").

39. Division of Aging and Adult Services, *Protective Services for Adults*, page III-58 (eff. date Apr. 1, 2011), https://ncdhhs.s3.amazonaws.com/s3fs-public/documents/files/APS_Manual.pdf.

Disclosure to Comply with Mandatory Reporting and Notification Requirements

Several laws require DSS to disclose APS information at various points in time. The burden is on DSS to initiate the following disclosures:

- *Notice to reporter (complainant).* When DSS receives a report of suspected abuse, neglect, or exploitation, the agency will conduct an evaluation. At the conclusion of the evaluation, the agency is required to immediately notify the person who filed the report about the outcome.[40] The notification must state whether the report was substantiated and whether services are being provided, but it must not include specific findings of the evaluation. DSS must document when and how (oral or written) it provided this required notice.[41]
- *APS register.* DSS is required to submit certain information to the Adult Protective Services Register, which is maintained by NC DHHS. The information submitted to the register by the counties is confidential.[42]
- *Residential facilities.* If the person who is the subject of the APS report is in a residential care facility, such as a nursing home, DSS is required to provide specific information to the facility's administrator after conducting the evaluation.[43]

---

40. 10A NCAC 71A .0202. At the time of the report, DSS should ask the reporter if he or she wants to receive this notification orally or in writing.

41. 10A NCAC 71A .0907.

42. 10A NCAC 71A .0806.

43. 10A NCAC 71A .0502.

Relevant Statute
North Carolina General Statutes

§ 108A-116.   Production of customers' financial records in cases of suspected financial exploitation; immunity; records may not be used against account owner.

(a) An investigating entity may, under the conditions specified in this section, petition the district court to issue a subpoena directing a financial institution to provide to the investigating entity the financial records of a disabled adult or older adult customer. The petition shall be filed in the county of residence of the disabled adult or older adult customer whose financial records are being subpoenaed. The court shall hear the case within two business days after the filing of the petition. The court shall issue the subpoena upon finding that all of the following conditions are met:

(1)   The investigating entity is investigating, pursuant to the investigating entity's statutory authority, a credible report that the disabled adult or older adult is being or has been financially exploited.

(2)   The disabled adult's or older adult's financial records are needed in order to substantiate or evaluate the report.

(3)   Time is of the essence in order to prevent further exploitation of that disabled adult or older adult.

(b) Delivery of the subpoena may be effected by hand, via certified mail, return receipt requested, or through a designated delivery service authorized pursuant to 26 U.S.C. § 7502(f)(2) and may be addressed to the financial institution's local branch or office vice president, its local branch or office manager or assistant branch or office manager, or the agent for service of process listed by the financial institution with the North Carolina Secretary of State or, if there is none, with the agent for service of process listed by the financial institution in any state in which it is domiciled.

(b1) A financial institution may challenge the subpoena by filing a motion to quash or modify the subpoena within ten days after receipt of delivery of the subpoena pursuant to subsection (b) of this section. The subpoena may be challenged only for the following reasons:

(1)   There is a procedural defect with the subpoena.

(2)   The subpoena contains insufficient information to identify the records subject to the subpoena.

(3)   The financial institution is otherwise prevented from promptly complying with the subpoena.

(4)   The petition was filed or subpoena requested for an improper purpose or based upon insufficient grounds.

(5)   The subpoena subjects the financial institution to an undue burden or is otherwise unreasonable or oppressive.

Within two business days after the motion is filed, the court shall hear the motion and issue an order upholding, modifying, or quashing the subpoena.

(c) Upon receipt of a subpoena delivered pursuant to subsection (b) of this section identifying the disabled adult or older adult customer or, if the subpoena is challenged pursuant to subsection (b1) of this section, entry of a court order upholding or modifying a subpoena, a financial institution shall promptly provide to the head of an investigating entity, or his or her designated agent, the financial records of a disabled adult or older adult customer.

(d) All produced copies of the disabled adult's or older adult's financial records, as well as any information obtained pursuant to the duty to report found in G.S. 108A-115, shall be kept confidential by the investigating entity unless required by court order to be disclosed to a party to a court proceeding or introduced and admitted into evidence in an open court proceeding.

(e) No financial institution or investigating entity, or officer or employee thereof, who acts in good faith in providing, seeking, or obtaining financial records or any other information in accordance with this section, or in providing testimony in any judicial proceeding based upon the contents thereof, may be held liable in any action for doing so.

(f) No customer may be subject to indictment, criminal prosecution, criminal punishment, or criminal penalty by reason of or on account of anything disclosed by a financial institution pursuant to this section, nor may any information obtained through such disclosure be used as evidence against the customer in any criminal or civil proceeding. Notwithstanding the foregoing, information obtained may be used against a person who is a joint account owner accused of financial exploitation of a disabled adult or older adult joint account holder, but solely for criminal or civil proceedings directly related to the alleged financial exploitation of the disabled adult or older adult joint account holder.

(g) The petition and the court's entire record of the proceedings under this section is not a matter of public record. Records qualifying under this subsection shall be maintained separately from other records, shall be withheld from public inspection, and may be examined only by order of the court. (2013-337, s. 4; 2014-115, s. 44(a).)

Relevant Regulations
North Carolina Administrative Code
TITLE 10A—HEALTH AND HUMAN SERVICES
CHAPTER 71—ADULT AND FAMILY SUPPORT
SUBCHAPTER 71A—PROTECTIVE SERVICES FOR ADULTS

SECTION .0500—RESIDENTIAL CARE FACILITIES

10A NCAC 71A .0501   GENERAL REQUIREMENT

(a) In accordance with provisions of G.S. 108A103 and the rules in Section .0200 of this Subchapter, the department of social services in the county in which the facility is located shall evaluate reports of abused, neglected, or exploited disabled adults in need of protective services who are specifically named patients or residents of nursing, combination, and residential care facilities. This includes reports regarding patients or residents who are placed from other counties.

(b) Complaints received by the county department of social services regarding general conditions or violations of standards in nursing and combination facilities and residential care facilities licensed under G.S. 122C shall be referred to the Division of Health Service Regulation.

(c) Complaints received by the county department of social services regarding general conditions or violations of standards in residential care facilities licensed under G.S. 131D2 shall be followed up by the adult home specialist in accordance with the specialist's ongoing responsibility for supervision of these facilities.

10A NCAC 71A .0502   NOTICE TO ADMINISTRATOR

(a) The county director will not inform the administrator prior to the first visit to the facility that a protective services report has been received, except in specific instances where the county director thinks the assistance of the administrator will be needed in conducting the evaluation.

(b) The county director shall provide the administrator of a nursing, combination, or residential care facility with a written summary of the nature of the protective services report, whether or not evidence of abuse, neglect or exploitation was found, and whether or not a need for protective services was substantiated. The written summary to the administrator shall be limited to the following:

   (1)   acknowledgement that a protective services report was received on a specified patient or resident of the facility;

   (2)   the specific allegations in the report (the complainant shall not be named);

   (3)   whether or not evidence of abuse, neglect or exploitation was found;

   (4)   whether or not the need for protective services was substantiated;

   (5)   a general statement as to how the conclusion was reached (the names of persons who were contacted during the evaluation to obtain information shall not be given).

10A NCAC 71A .0503   REPORT TO REGULATORY AGENCIES

(a) A copy of the written report required by Rule .0901 of this Subchapter shall be sent to the Division of Health Service Regulation, within 30 days of completion of the evaluation. If the identity of the person making the protective services report and the names of individuals who provide information about the disabled adult are needed by the Division of Health Service Regulation in order to carry out an investigation, that information shall be shared verbally with the Division on request.

(b) When evidence of financial exploitation is found in Medicaid funded facilities, the county department of social services shall send a copy of the written report to the Division of Medical Assistance, as well as to the Division of Health Service Regulation.

(c) When, in the course of an evaluation, evidence of abuse, neglect or exploitation is found, the county director shall notify the Division of Health Service Regulation immediately by telephone. In addition the county director shall inform the Division of Health Service Regulation as to whether or not the need for protective services will be substantiated.

(d) When, in the course of an evaluation, it appears that a report of a need for protective services will not be substantiated, but the county director finds violations of licensure standards, such violations shall be reported immediately to the appropriate supervisory agency. Reports of violations of standards in nursing and combination facilities and residential care facilities licensed under G.S. 122C shall be made to the Division of Health Service Regulation. Reports of violations of standards in residential care facilities licensed under G.S. 131D2 shall be made to the adult home specialist in the county department of social services.

SECTION .0600—STATE MENTAL HEALTH: MENTAL RETARDATION: SUBSTANCE ABUSE SERVICES INSTITUTIONS

10A NCAC 71A .0601   EVALUATIONS OF ABUSE: NEGLECT AND EXPLOITATION

(a) The county department of social services shall initiate its evaluation in accordance with the time frame in Rule .0204 of this Subchapter.

(b) When the report comes from a source other than the facility administration, the county department shall inform the chief administrator of the involved facility of the report as appropriate and of applicable state law.

(c) The county department shall notify the complainant that the department is making an evaluation.

(d) Upon completion of the evaluation, the department shall set forth its findings and proposed actions in writing to:

   (1)   the chief administrator of the involved facility;
   (2)   the disabled adult's legal guardian, if any.

10A NCAC 71A .0602   REPORTS OF NEED FOR MEDICAL TREATMENT FOR RESIDENTS

(a) Rules in Section .0200 of this Subchapter shall be followed by the county department of social services in carrying out the evaluation of reports of need for medical treatment made in accordance with G.S. 108A101(m).

(b) After completing the evaluation, if it is reasonably determined that the person needs protective services, the county department shall petition the district court and request a hearing on the matter. The petition must present the need for specific medical treatment, as well as other circumstances substantiating neglect and request that an individual or organization be designated to consent to the medical treatment. If an emergency exists, the department shall petition the district court for an order to provide emergency services.

(c) After the court's decision is made, the county department shall send to the institution the findings of the court.

(d) When the county department is designated by the court, the director or his designee shall verbally communicate to the institution consent for medical treatment. This shall be done immediately after the judgment is made, to be followed by written consent.

SECTION .0800—CONFIDENTIALITY

10A NCAC 71A .0801   COLLATERAL CONTACTS

Collateral contacts with persons knowledgeable about a disabled adult's situation may be made without the adult or caretaker's consent when such contacts are necessary to complete a protective services evaluation.

10A NCAC 71A .0802   IDENTITY OF COMPLAINANT AND OF INDIVIDUALS WHO HAVE KNOWLEDGE OF THE SITUATION

The identity of the complainant and of individuals who have knowledge of the situation of the disabled adult shall be kept confidential unless the court requires that such persons' identities be revealed with the exceptions that:

(1) the complainant's name and the names of individuals who have knowledge of the situation of the disabled adult may be given verbally to the Division of Health Service Regulation when requested by that agency in order to carry out its investigation, and

(2) to the District Attorney's office and to law enforcement agencies which are prosecuting or conducting a criminal investigation of alleged abuse, neglect or exploitation of a disabled adult.

10A NCAC 71A .0803   SPECIFIC FINDINGS

Specific findings of the evaluation shall be kept confidential and shall not be released without consent of the disabled adult or court order, except that the department of social services at its discretion may share information about the adult with other persons or agencies without the adult or caretaker's consent to the extent necessary to provide protective services. When evidence of abuse, neglect, or exploitation is found, and upon request of the district attorney or law enforcement agencies, such information shall be sent to help with a criminal investigation or prosecution of abuse, neglect or exploitation.

10A NCAC 71A .0804   REFERRAL TO ANOTHER COUNTY

When a client who is receiving protective services under court order moves from one county to another, a protective services referral may be made by the first county to the second county without the client's consent. When the second county requests information in order to conduct its evaluation, the first county shall provide the needed information, including all information about the protective services report, results of the evaluation, and services provided to remedy the protective services problem.

10A NCAC 71A .0805   RELEASE OF SPECIFIC FINDINGS TO OTHER GOVERNMENTAL AGENCIES

Federal, state, and law enforcement agencies may be sent copies of the written report as specified in Rule .0901 of this Subchapter when the results of the adult protective services evaluation indicate violations of statutes, rules, or regulations enforced by these agencies.

10A NCAC 71A .0806   ADULT PROTECTIVE SERVICES REGISTER

(a) Information submitted by county departments of social services to the Adult Protective Services Register is confidential. Non-identifying statistical information and general information about the scope, nature and extent of adult abuse, neglect and exploitation in North Carolina is not subject to this Rule of confidentiality.

(b) Access to the Adult Protective Services Register is restricted to:
  (1)   the county department of social services,
        (A)   in order to identify whether an adult who is the subject of an Adult Protective Services evaluation has been previously reported and evaluated under G.S. 108A, Article 6 in any county in the state; or
        (B)   in order to share client specific information with an out of state protective services agency to assure that protective services will be made available to an adult previously served in North Carolina as quickly as possible for the purpose of preventing further abuse, neglect or exploitation; or
        (C)   in order to share client specific information with law enforcement agencies to assure that protective services will be made available to an adult as quickly as possible;
  (2)   the Division of Social Services staff,
        (A)   in order to perform duties pertinent to managing and maintaining the Register and monitoring, auditing, evaluating or facilitating the administration of other state and federal programs regarding Adult Protective Services based on information in the Register, or

  (B) in order to share client specific information with an out of state protective services agency to assure that protective services will be made available to an adult previously served in North Carolina as quickly as possible for the purpose of preventing further abuse, neglect or exploitation; and

(3) individuals who receive approval to conduct studies of cases in the Adult Protective Services Register.

  (A) Such approval must be requested in writing to the Director, Division of Social Services. The written request will specify and be approved on the basis of:

    (i) an explanation of how the findings of the study have potential for expanding knowledge and improving professional practices in the area of prevention, identification and treatment of adult abuse, neglect and exploitation;

    (ii) a description of how the study will be conducted and how the findings will be used;

    (iii) a presentation of the individual's credentials; and

    (iv) a description of how the individual will safeguard the information.

  (B) Access will be denied when in the judgment of the Director the study will have minimal impact on either knowledge or practice.

SECTION .0900—DOCUMENTATION AND REPORTS

10A NCAC 71A .0901 WRITTEN REPORT OF THE EVALUATION

(a) Written reports shall be completed when:

(1) the adult protective services evaluation was conducted on a patient or resident of a facility as defined in G.S. 131E 101, 131D 2(a)(3), or 122C; or

(2) evidence of abuse, neglect or exploitation is found.

(b) After completing the evaluation, the written report shall be compiled, including the following information:

(1) the name, address, age and condition of the adult;

(2) the allegations (the written report shall not include the identity of the person making the complaint);

(3) the evaluation including the agency's findings and supporting documents (e.g. psychological, medical report);

(4) conclusions;

(5) recommendations for action.

10A NCAC 71A .0906 REPORT TO DISTRICT ATTORNEY

Notification to the district attorney in accordance with G.S. 108A 109 shall be in written form and shall include the information specified in Rule .0901 of this Section.

10A NCAC 71A .0907   REPORT TO THE COMPLAINANT

(a) The required notice to the complainant may be oral or in writing at the discretion of the complainant and shall be made immediately on completing the evaluation. It shall include a statement of whether or not the report was substantiated and, if so, a statement that the agency is providing continued services.

(b) Documentation shall be made of when and how the notice is given.

(c) In order to protect the client's confidentiality, the notice shall not include specific findings of the evaluation.

Chapter 4

Child Protective Services

County social services agencies provide a wide array of services to protect children and support families.[1] Much of the time, the agency becomes involved with a child or family because it has received a report that a child may have been abused or neglected, is dependent, or has died as a result of maltreatment.[2]

This chapter uses the term "child protective services" or CPS to refer to the services that an agency may provide when protecting a child or working with a family after receiving such a report. Protective services may include, for example, screening reports, providing in-home services and support for the family, or removing a child from a home. This chapter does not use the broader term "child welfare" because it does not address the full complement of child-related services provided by county agencies, including adoption and financial assistance for foster placements. Those programs are subject to different confidentiality laws. This chapter also does not address confi-

---

1. N.C. GEN. STAT. (hereinafter G.S.) § 7B-300 ("Protective services shall include the screening of reports, the performance of an assessment using either a family assessment response or an investigative assessment response, casework, or other counseling services to parents, guardians, or other caretakers as provided by the director to help the parents, guardians, or other caretakers and the court to prevent abuse or neglect, to improve the quality of child care, to be more adequate parents, guardians, or caretakers, and to preserve and stabilize family life.").

2. For more information about the reporting law, see JANET MASON, REPORTING CHILD ABUSE AND NEGLECT IN NORTH CAROLINA (UNC School of Government, 2013).

dentiality of information about children who are involved with the juvenile delinquency system but not with the child protective services program.[3]

When a county department of social services (DSS) receives a report, the director has a duty to conduct an assessment.[4] In the course of the assessment, the director or the director's designee will gather a lot of information about the situation and the people involved. The information collected by the agency can be extraordinarily sensitive and is therefore subject to multiple layers of federal and state confidentiality laws.

This chapter is designed to answer only one question:

> When may DSS disclose identifiable CPS information without authorization?

It will provide an overview of the legal landscape in this area, summarize applicable federal and state laws, and discuss how to interpret and apply the combination of laws, including Section 108A-80 of the North Carolina General Statutes (hereinafter G.S.), in several key areas related to CPS programs.

Overview of the Legal Landscape

There is a complex web of laws that apply to social services information in the CPS area. Several federal and state statutes and regulations require DSS to keep CPS information confidential and specify when confidential information may be disclosed. As discussed in Chapter 1, multiple laws may apply in each specific situation, and it can be difficult to know whether a disclosure is allowed.

---

3. *See* Janet Mason, *Confidentiality in Juvenile Delinquency Proceedings*, JUVENILE LAW BULLETIN No. 2011/01 (May 2011); UNC School of Government, *North Carolina Juvenile Justice-Behavioral Health Information Sharing Guide* (Apr. 2015), www.sog.unc.edu/sites/www.sog.unc.edu/files/JJBH%20Information%20Sharing%20Guide%20FINAL_4.7.15.pdf.

4. G.S. 7B-302(a); N.C. ADMIN. CODE (hereinafter NCAC) title 10A, ch. 70A, § .0105. Different timelines and duties apply to assessments based upon the type of report filed.

There are some fundamental concepts to keep in mind when trying to weave all of these laws together:

- G.S. 108A-80 applies to CPS records. Other state laws apply to CPS records as well.
- If G.S. 108A-80 allows a disclosure but the other applicable state laws do not, the information should not be disclosed.
- Federal laws apply to most CPS records.
- If federal law *requires* disclosure, DSS should disclose the information.
- If state law *requires* disclosure, DSS should disclose the information only if federal law allows disclosure.
- If federal law does not allow disclosure, DSS should not disclose the information.
- If federal law allows (but does not require) disclosure but state law does not allow disclosure, DSS should not disclose the information.

Below is a brief discussion of the key federal and state laws that apply, followed by a discussion of how DSS should interpret and apply these laws together when deciding whether to disclose information in the course of providing protective services to children.

Federal Law

At the federal level, there are laws that place conditions on states' receipt of federal funds for child protective services. Several of the conditions tied to funding provided through the Child Abuse Prevention and Treatment Act (CAPTA) and Title IV of the Social Security Act (Title IV) relate to confidentiality.

CAPTA

One of the most comprehensive federal laws that applies is the Child Abuse Prevention and Treatment Act, or CAPTA.[5] It applies to all CPS records and requires the state to

- preserve the confidentiality of CPS records "in order to protect the rights of the child and of the child's parents or guardians";

---

5. 42 U.S.C. § 5106a.

- allow disclosure of confidential information in limited circumstances, such as to the individual who is the subject of the report, to child fatality review teams, and to the court;
- require disclosure of confidential CPS information to governmental entities (or their agents) when necessary to carry out the entities' legal duty to protect children from abuse and neglect; and
- allow public disclosure of information about any case of child abuse or neglect that results in a child fatality or near fatality.[6]

While this list appears restrictive, there is another provision that defers to state law. It allows disclosures to "other entities or classes of individuals statutorily authorized by the State to receive such information pursuant to a legitimate State purpose."[7] Therefore, it is unlikely that CAPTA's confidentiality protections will be more restrictive than those authorized by state statute.

One could argue that because CAPTA defers to "statutorily authorized" disclosures, those disclosures authorized *only* by regulation are preempted (or prohibited). On the other hand, because regulations must be based upon authority granted by statute,[8] any disclosure authorized by regulation is also technically authorized by statute. For example, one of the regulations in Chapter 69 of Title 10A of the North Carolina Administrative Code (hereinafter NCAC) allows disclosures for research in some circumstances.[9] (See Chapter 2). This specific regulation was promulgated by the Social Services Commission based upon the general confidentiality provisions and delegated rulemaking authority in G.S. 108A-80. The most reasonable interpretation of this "statutorily authorized" language in CAPTA would be that it encompasses not only statutory language but also regulations that are lawfully promulgated pursuant to statutory authority. Therefore, CAPTA would allow DSS to make disclosures that are authorized by regulation even if they are not specifically mentioned in a statute.

---

6. 42 U.S.C. § 5106a(b)(2)(vii)–(x).

7. 42 U.S.C. § 5106a(b)(2)(viii)(VI).

8. Rulemaking bodies may only adopt regulations within the scope of their delegated authority. G.S. 150B-19.1(a)(1) ("An agency may adopt only rules that are expressly authorized by federal or State law and that are necessary to serve the public interest.").

9. 10A NCAC 69 .0502.

Title IV of the Social Security Act

A different federal law adds another layer of protection to some CPS-related information. Title IV of the Social Security Act includes several distinct parts, each of which outlines the requirements that attach to particular federal funding streams.[10] Two parts are directly related to child welfare programs administered by county departments of social services:

- Part B (IV-B) governs funding streams that support child welfare related services and administrative functions.[11]
- Part E (IV-E) governs funding streams that support foster care and adoption assistance programs.[12]

In order to receive federal funding under Title IV-B or Title IV-E, the state must submit a plan to the federal government that demonstrates compliance with all federal requirements.[13]

One of the requirements is that the state plan comply with the confidentiality restrictions that are included in the regulations governing a completely different federal program—Temporary Assistance for Needy Families (in North Carolina, the program is known as Work First).[14] The state has

---

10. 42 U.S.C. §§ 601–87.

11. For more information about Title IV-B funding, see Emilie Stoltzfus, *Child Welfare: Funding for Child and Family Services Authorized Under Title IV-B of the Social Security Act*, Congressional Research Service (Oct. 29, 2014), http://greenbook.waysandmeans.house.gov/sites/greenbook.waysandmeans.house.gov/files/R41860_gb.pdf.

12. For more information about Title IV-E funding, see Emilie Stoltzfus, *Child Welfare: State Plan Requirements under the Title IV-E Foster Care, Adoption Assistance, and Kinship Guardianship Assistance Program*, Congressional Research Service (Nov. 17, 2014), http://greenbook.waysandmeans.house.gov/sites/greenbook.waysandmeans.house.gov/files/R42794_gb_0.pdf.

13. The state plan requirements under Title IV-B do not address confidentiality directly. There is, however, a federal regulation that requires the state plan for Title IV-B to comply with the same confidentiality requirements that apply to Title IV-E. *See* 45 C.F.R. § 1355.21(a) (requiring state plans for both IV-B and IV-E to comply with 42 U.S.C. § 671(a)(8)).

14. 45 C.F.R. § 1355.21(b) (requiring compliance with US Department of Health and Human Services regulations listed in 45 C.F.R. § 1355.30; one of the regulations listed is 45 C.F.R. § 205.50, the TANF confidentiality provisions). Those same regulations apply to many other federal programs, including Medicaid.

authority to implement and enforce these confidentiality requirements in the context of programs receiving Title IV-E funding.[15]

The state plans typically identify the state confidentiality laws that, when taken together, satisfy the federal requirements. For example, the state's Title IV-E plan identifies more than forty state statutes and regulations.[16] The state's plans, including the confidentiality provisions, are consistently approved by the federal authorities, and therefore it seems reasonable to assume that the state's confidentiality laws substantially conform to the expectations of the federal funding agencies. It is important to remember, however, that if a disclosure is *allowed* by state law but *not allowed* by federal law, the information should not be disclosed.

In summary, federal law allows DSS to disclose information connected to the Title IV-B and Title IV-E programs only as follows:

- to administer the two Title IV programs as well as many other federally funded programs (administrative functions include establishing eligibility, determining the amount of assistance, and providing services for applicants and recipients);[17]
- for the investigation, prosecution, or criminal or civil proceeding conducted in connection with the administration of any of those federally funded programs;[18]
- for the administration of any other federal or federally assisted program that provides assistance or services directly to individuals on the basis of need;[19]

15. 45 C.F.R. § 205.50(ii).

16. Plan for Title IV-E of the Social Security Act; Federal Payments for Foster Care and Adoption Assistance; State of North Carolina (Sept. 2012) (on file with author).

17. 42 U.S.C. § 671 (a)(8)(A); 45 C.F.R. § 205.50(a)(1)(i)(A). These three administrative activities are included in the regulation and are most likely examples rather than an exclusive list of authorized activities. *See also* Social Services; Public Assistance; Confidentiality of Records; Fraud Investigations by Law Enforcement Officers, 53 N.C. Op. Att'y Gen. 108 (June 5, 1984) (relying on similar language to authorize disclosure of public assistance and social services records to law enforcement officials who are investigating program fraud).

18. 42 U.S.C. § 671(a)(8)(B); 45 C.F.R. § 205.50(a)(1)(i)(B).

19. 42 U.S.C. § 671(a)(8)(C); 45 C.F.R. § 205.50(a)(1)(i)(C).

- in connection with any legally authorized audit or similar activity conducted in connection with the administration of the Title IV programs;[20]
- for the administration of a state unemployment compensation program;[21]
- in order to report and provide information to appropriate authorities with respect to known or suspected child abuse or neglect;[22] and
- to assist law enforcement officials in locating a fugitive.[23]

Note that this list of authorized disclosures does *not* include language similar to the CAPTA language deferring to disclosures authorized by state statute. Therefore, DSS should not disclose information when disclosure is authorized by state statute or regulation but not allowed by this federal law (Title IV).[24] For example, a state regulation allows disclosures for research.[25]

_____

20. 42 U.S.C. § 671(a)(8)(D); 45 C.F.R. § 205.50(a)(1)(i)(E).

21. 45 C.F.R. § 205.50(a)(1)(i)(F).

22. 42 U.S.C. § 671(a)(8)(E); 42 U.S.C. § 671(9); 45 C.F.R. § 205.50(a)(1)(i)(G). The Title IV-E statute allows broader information sharing with respect to child abuse and neglect than the federal regulations.

23. 45 C.F.R. § 205.50(a)(1)(v). DSS may share a recipient's current address with a law enforcement official if (1) the official requests the information, (2) the official provides the recipient's name and Social Security number, and (3) the official "satisfactorily demonstrates" that the recipient is a fugitive felon, the official has a duty to apprehend the fugitive, and the request is being made in connection with that duty.

24. Guidance from the federal government explains:

> There may be instances where CPS information is subject both to disclosure requirements under CAPTA and to the confidentiality requirements under title IV-E and 45 C.F.R. 205.50. To the extent that the CAPTA provisions require disclosure (such as in section 106 (b)(2)(B)(ix)), the CAPTA disclosure provision would prevail in the event of a conflict since the CAPTA confidentiality provisions were most recently enacted. Where the CAPTA provision is permissive (such as in sections 106 (b)(2)(B)(viii)(I)-(VI)), it allows States to disclose such information without violating CAPTA, but it does not make such disclosure permissible in other programs if it is not otherwise allowed under the other program's governing statute or regulations.

U.S. Department of Health and Human Services, Administration for Children and Families, Child Welfare Policy Manual, Sec. 8.4E, Question 6 (Sept. 28, 2011), www.acf.hhs.gov/cwpm/programs/cb/laws_policies/laws/cwpm/qaHistory.jsp?citID=56&id=767.

25. 10A NCAC § 69 .0502.

Because the confidentiality laws connected to Title IV do not allow that type of disclosure, any information from programs that receive Title IV-B or Title IV-E funding should not be disclosed to researchers pursuant to that state regulation.

The confidentiality laws connected to these two Title IV programs apply to much of the CPS information maintained by DSS, including names and addresses of individuals served by the programs, information about their "social and economic conditions or circumstances," information about DSS's evaluation, and medical information.[26]

Interestingly, one regulation expressly prohibits "disclosure of any information that identifies an individual receiving assistance or services by name or address to any Federal, State, or local committee or legislative body" unless it is allowed in connection with a legally authorized audit or similar activity.[27] See the discussion at the end of this chapter regarding disclosing information to members of social services boards acting in an oversight capacity.

State Law

At the state level, several different laws must be considered when evaluating whether DSS is required or allowed to disclose information in a particular circumstance. The starting point will be G.S. 108A-80 and the accompanying regulations in 10A NCAC 69 (Chapter 69 regulations). As discussed in Chapter 2, these state laws require DSS to protect client information but allow it to disclose information without authorization in several circumstances, including

- to the state for purposes of program supervision and reporting,
- to other county departments of social services,
- to researchers,
- to other governmental entities for purposes of accountability and administration,
- pursuant to a court order, and
- in order to comply with other laws.

In addition to G.S. 108A-80 and the Chapter 69 regulations, several other state laws are specific to CPS records and can be interpreted as being more

---

26. 45 C.F.R. § 205.50(2)(i).
27. 45 C.F.R. § 205.50(iii).

restrictive in some ways than those overarching laws and regulations. If a disclosure is allowed by G.S. 108A-80 but not allowed by these CPS-specific confidentiality laws, DSS should not disclose.

The primary CPS-specific confidentiality laws are

- G.S. 7B-302(a1), which applies broadly to all information received by DSS in connection with its child protective services work;
- G.S. 7B-2901(a), which applies to court records of juvenile cases involving allegations of abuse, neglect, and dependency;
- G.S. 7B-2901(b), which applies to DSS records of abused, neglected, or dependent children who are in the department's protective custody or who have been placed with the department pursuant to a court order;
- 10A NCAC 70A .0113, which is based on the authority in the two statutes above and applies to "protective services records" as described in a different regulation, 10A NCAC 70A .0112; and
- G.S. 7B-3100, which applies to information sharing among "designated agencies" serving children receiving protective services or involved in a juvenile court proceeding.

Each of these laws is discussed in more detail below.

G.S. 7B-302(a1)

The first law establishes a baseline of protection for all of the information that DSS receives related to these children and specifies when that information may be released. It applies as soon as DSS receives a report of suspected abuse, neglect, dependency, or death due to maltreatment. The information contained in the report, the reporter's identity, and information gathered by DSS in the course of assessing the report are all confidential pursuant to this law. The statute, in fact, says that the information "shall be held in strictest confidence" and may be released in only a few circumstances.

G.S. 7B-2901(a)

This law governs the juvenile case record that is maintained by the clerk of court. It outlines the information that must be included in the court's record: the summons, petition, custody order, court order, written motions, recordings of hearings, and other papers filed in the proceeding.

The record may be released pursuant to a court order. In addition, the following individuals and agencies are allowed to examine and obtain copies of the written parts of the record:

- the juvenile named in the petition;
- the juvenile's guardian ad litem;
- DSS;
- the juvenile's parent, guardian, or custodian; and
- the attorney for the juvenile or the juvenile's parent, guardian, or custodian.

When DSS has or receives a copy of information that is part of the court's record, it is reasonable to assume that DSS should follow the same restrictions on disclosure. This can present challenges for DSS because the agency may wish to share some of this information, such as a court order, with another person or agency in the course of carrying out its legal duties and responsibilities.

G.S. 7B-2901(b)

This law is similar to G.S. 7B-302 but is narrower in scope in two ways. First, it applies to information about a smaller group of children: those who are in protective custody or who have been placed with DSS by a court. It does not apply, for example, to information gathered when DSS has evaluated a child's situation based on a report of suspected abuse or neglect but concluded that no abuse or neglect occurred. It also does not apply where a voluntary service plan has been executed between the parent and DSS. Second, G.S. 7B-2901(b) concerns only a subset of the information maintained by DSS because it applies to a "record" rather than "all information received" by DSS. According to the statute, the record includes

- family background information;
- reports of social, medical, psychiatric, or psychological information concerning a child or the child's family;
- interviews with the child's family; or
- other information that the court finds should be protected from public inspection "in the best interests" of the child.

Like G.S. 7B-302, this law specifies when the information may be disclosed by DSS.

10A NCAC 70A .0113

This regulation is based on authority from the two statutes described above, G.S. 7B-302 and G.S. 7B-2901. It limits disclosure of information in the "protective services case record," which DSS is required to create when (1) the agency initiates protective services for a child or (2) a child is placed in DSS custody by the court.[28] This regulation is extremely strict and allows disclosure in very limited circumstances. It must, however, be read and interpreted together with other applicable laws that may require or authorize disclosure. For example, this regulation does not authorize disclosing information to foster parents, but a federal law requires DSS to disclose certain health and educational information to them.[29] DSS must consider all relevant laws, not only this regulation or another law, when deciding whether to disclose information in a particular circumstance.

G.S. 7B-3100 and the Accompanying Regulations

This statute and the accompanying regulations[30] allow "designated agencies" that are providing services to a child to share information more readily. An agency is a designated agency if it is listed in a state regulation[31] or is a local agency identified in an administrative order issued by a chief district court judge.[32] The regulations specifically include county departments of social services. Designated agencies must share confidential information

---

28. 10A NCAC 70A .0112 (contents of protective services record); *see also* NC DIVISION OF SOCIAL SERVICES, FAMILY SERVICES MANUAL, Vol. I, Ch. VIII, Sec. 1424, Case Record (Jan. 2007), http://info.dhhs.state.nc.us/olm/manuals/dss/csm-60/man/pdf%20docs/CS1424.pdf. Note that this "protective services record" is more extensive than the DSS "record" that is governed by G.S. 7B-2901(b).

29. 42 U.S.C. § 671 (a)(16) (requiring a case plan); 42 U.S.C. § 675(1)(C) (health and education records that must be included in case plan); 42 U.S.C. § 675(5)(D) (requiring that the health and education information be shared with foster families). *See also* 45 C.F.R. § 1356.21(f) and (h) (detailing requirements for the case plan and case plan review).

30. 14B NCAC 11A .0301–.0302.

31. 14B NCAC 11A .0301.

32. The implementing regulation, which was issued by the NC Department of Public Safety, Division of Adult Correction and Juvenile Justice, lists the designated agencies. Included on that list is "a local agency designated by an administrative order issued by the chief district court judge of the district court district in which the agency is located, as an agency authorized to share information pursuant to these Rules and the standards set forth in G.S. 7B-3100." 14B NCAC 11A .0301.

with other designated agencies that request it. Information so shared may be used only

- for the protection of the juvenile and others or
- to improve the educational opportunities of the juvenile.

These are important limitations. The law does not give public agencies free rein to share information for any purpose. In addition, agencies that receive information pursuant to this law must keep it confidential.

There are obviously several laws that need to be considered when deciding when to disclose CPS information. At a minimum, DSS must consider applicable federal laws, G.S. 108A-80 and the accompanying regulations in Chapter 69, G.S. 7B-302, and 10A NCAC 70A .0113. If there has been a juvenile court proceeding or a juvenile is in DSS custody, DSS will also need to consider G.S. 7B-2901(b). The rest of this chapter will integrate the analysis of all of these laws by

- identifying information subject to heightened protections on disclosure,
- discussing the applicable laws for several specific types of disclosures, and
- highlighting disclosures that are required by state law.

Heightened Protection for Identities

Some of the most sensitive information DSS maintains includes the identities of people who submit protective services reports and of other people who offer information to DSS in connection with assessments. Revealing a person's identity could put that individual or others at risk or compromise the assessment process. For that reason, state law provides heightened protection for the types of information discussed below.

Identity of the Reporter

The identity of the person who submits a protective services report is subject to heightened confidentiality protections under state law as follows:

- *The identity must be disclosed to a government entity with a court order.* DSS *must* disclose information regarding the identity of the reporter to a government entity (or its agent) if a court issues an order directing the agency to do so.[33] A court may, for example, order the director to reveal the identity of a reporter at a hearing on a petition alleging that someone has obstructed or interfered with an assessment of a report of abuse, neglect, or dependency.[34]

- *The identity may be disclosed to a government entity without a court order.* In the absence of a court order, DSS *may* disclose information regarding the identity of the reporter to a government entity (or its agent) if the entity "demonstrates a need for the reporter's name to carry out the entity's mandated responsibilities."[35] In this situation, the burden is on the entity requesting the information to (1) demonstrate the need for the name and (2) explain how the need relates to the entity's mandated responsibilities. It is within DSS's discretion to evaluate the request and determine whether it should disclose the identity of the reporter. While the facts surrounding these types of requests will likely vary widely, DSS should develop a general policy for evaluating these requests and making decisions about disclosure.

There are two other laws that address disclosure of the reporter's identity. The first provides that DSS is not allowed to share the identity of the reporter with the parties to a juvenile proceeding in the course of discovery.[36] The second, which allows DSS to file a petition asserting that a person is interfering with or obstructing a protective services assessment, authorizes the court to order DSS to disclose the reporter's identity.[37]

One could argue that a judge has the inherent authority to order disclosure of the reporter's identity in other circumstances if necessary to the

---

33. G.S. 7B-302(a1)(1a).

34. G.S. 7B-303.

35. 7B-302(a1)(1a). *See also* 10A NCAC 70A .0105(c) (authorizing DSS to disclose the identity of the reporter to law enforcement officials in connection with a referral of a potential crime).

36. G.S. 7B-700(a). This law authorizes DSS to share information with parties in the course of discovery but states that "this subsection does not authorize the disclosure of the identity of the report or any uniquely identifying information that would lead to the discovery of the reporter's identity in accordance with G.S. 7B-302 . . . ."

37. G.S. 7B-303(e).

proper administration of justice.[38] The counterargument—and probably the stronger argument—is that the legislature considered this issue and took action to limit DSS's ability to share the identity, thus foreclosing any possibility of a judge exercising such authority.[39]

Identity of Others

After a petition has been filed in a juvenile proceeding, the parties to the proceeding will participate in the discovery process. In general, information sharing in this context is relatively open. DSS is authorized to share relevant information with parties but, as mentioned above, DSS is not allowed to disclose the identity of the reporter. In addition, DSS may not disclose the identity of any other person if it "determines that the disclosure would be likely to endanger the life or safety of the person."[40] If DSS is served with a motion seeking discovery of the identity of such a person, DSS should request a protective order, which allows the judge to consider the information *in camera* and evaluate the risks involved.[41]

Specific Types of Disclosures

This section will consider how to apply the various confidentiality laws in the context of disclosures

- allowed by G.S. 108A-80 and the Chapter 69 regulations,
- to government entities in order to protect the juvenile,
- to schools and designated agencies for education-related purposes,
- to the juvenile's guardian ad litem,
- to collateral sources,
- in a private civil case,
- to a child who is involved in a criminal or delinquency case, and
- from the central registry.

---

38. *See* Michael Crowell, *Inherent Authority* (Feb. 2014), www.sog.unc.edu/sites/www.sog.unc.edu/files/Inherent%20authority%20Feb%2014.pdf.

39. *See, e.g.*, State v. Hardy, 293 N.C. 105, 125 (1977) (". . . where a statute expressly restricts pretrial discovery, as does G.S. 15A-904(a), the trial court has no authority to order discovery.").

40. G.S. 7B-700(a).

41. G.S. 7B-700(d).

This is obviously not an exhaustive study of every type of disclosure that DSS may consider or be asked to make. Instead, it is a summary of some of the most common scenarios faced by county agencies.

It is important to remember that even if the federal and state laws discussed in this chapter allow the disclosure, it is possible that another more restrictive law may apply and prohibit the disclosure. For example, if information in the record is subject to the federal substance abuse confidentiality regulation,[42] DSS may be required to redact that information. See Chapter 5 for a discussion of the substance abuse confidentiality regulations.

Allowed by G.S. 108A-80 and the Chapter 69 Regulations

As discussed in Chapter 2, G.S. 108A-80 and the implementing regulations in Chapter 69 of the North Carolina Administrative Code allow DSS to disclose information without authorization

- to the state for purposes of supervision and reporting,
- to other county departments of social services,
- to other governmental entities for purposes of accountability and administration,
- to schools for education-related purposes,
- pursuant to a court order,
- to researchers, and
- in order to comply with other state and federal laws.

This body of law applies to CPS records.[43] But before proceeding with a disclosure that is allowed by G.S. 108A-80 and the Chapter 69 regulations, DSS must ensure that the disclosure is also allowed by the other CPS-specific federal and state confidentiality laws discussed in this chapter.

In short, most of the disclosures allowed by G.S. 108A-80 and the Chapter 69 regulations are also allowed by the applicable CPS-specific laws. A few provisions require some additional explanation.

---

42. 42 C.F.R. Part 2.

43. G.S. 108A-80 refers to both public assistance and social services programs. *See also* Social Services; Public Assistance; Confidentiality of Records; Fraud Investigations by Law Enforcement Officers, 53 N.C. Op. Att'y Gen. 108 (June 5, 1984) (explaining that the Chapter 69 regulations apply to social services programs to the same extent as public assistance programs).

To other Governmental Entities for Purposes of Accountability and Administration
This provision in the Chapter 69 regulations is extremely broad. It authorizes information sharing with other government agencies for "monitoring, auditing, evaluating, or facilitating the administration of other state and federal programs."[44] It requires that DSS evaluate the request and only make the disclosure if (1) the need for disclosure is justifiable for the purpose and (2) adequate safeguards are maintained to protect the information from re-disclosure.

This state regulation is not in conflict with CAPTA or Title IV, because both allow information sharing with other government programs for administrative purposes.[45] The regulations associated with Title IV also include language authorizing DSS to disclose limited information to law enforcement officials in order to locate a fugitive felon.[46]

One could argue, though, that the language in G.S. 7B-302 requiring that CPS information be held "in the strictest confidence" overrides the authority to make this type of disclosure.[47] In other words, because this type of disclosure is not allowed by any of the state's CPS-specific confidentiality laws, it should not be allowed based upon this general regulation in Chapter 69.

This area of the law is not clear. The most cautious approach DSS could take would be to refuse to disclose CPS information to other government programs for accountability and administration purposes. Such a conservative

---

44. 10A NCAC 69 .0503.

45. *See* 42 U.S.C. 5106(a)(b)(2)(B)(viii)(VI) (CAPTA provision allowing disclosure pursuant to state statute); 45 C.F.R. § 205.50(1)(i) (regulation aligned with Title IV that allows disclosures related to administration and auditing of government programs).

46. 45 C.F.R. § 205.50(a)(1)(v).

47. G.S. 7B-302(a1). A 1984 opinion from the North Carolina Attorney General's office did not adopt this interpretation. Instead, it concluded that disclosures from social services records would be allowed when needed for fraud investigations. Social Services; Public Assistance; Confidentiality of Records; Fraud Investigations by Law Enforcement Officers, 53 N.C. Op. Att'y Gen. 108 (June 5, 1984). That opinion was based on an earlier and less rigorous version of the state confidentiality laws. A later opinion interpreted the CPS-specific confidentiality laws in place at the time as prohibiting disclosures that were required by a state statute. North Carolina Department of Justice, Advisory Opinion: Access to Records by Social Services Boards, Letter to Kevin M. Fitzgerald, Director of the Division of Social Services (Apr. 20, 1995) (concluding that DSS must not disclose CPS records to governing board members despite a state statute granting them access).

interpretation could, however, impede delivery of services to children or families or prevent collaborations across government programs. Absent guidance from the state, DSS will need to work with its attorneys to decide how best to proceed.

To Researchers

The Chapter 69 regulations authorize disclosure for research purposes, as described in Chapter 2. The confidentiality regulations associated with Title IV do not allow disclosure for research purposes.[48] In addition, one could adopt the same position described above by asserting that the "strictest confidence" language in G.S. 7B-302(a1) prohibits these disclosures because they are not otherwise allowed by the state's CPS-specific confidentiality laws.

This area of the law also is not clear. The most cautious approach DSS could take would be to refuse to disclose CPS information to researchers without authorization. Alternatively, DSS could consider adopting policies regarding allowable disclosure of CPS-specific information for research purposes, consistent with the Chapter 69 regulations. If it does adopt such a policy, the agency should consider excluding information from programs receiving Title IV-B or Title IV-E funding.

To Government Entities in Order to Protect the Juvenile

G.S. 7B-302 requires that DSS disclose information to "any federal, State, or local government entity or its agent in order to protect a juvenile from abuse or neglect."[49] The requirement to disclose to government entities is extremely broad, but it relies on DSS to determine whether the disclosure would serve the purpose of protecting the child. In addition to allowing disclosure to law enforcement officials, schools, and state, county, municipal, and tribal government entities within North Carolina, this law allows disclosure to government entities in other states or to federal officials. According to guidance issued by the state, DSS may not rely upon this provision in the law to disclose information in "civil child custody cases between parents or

---

48. 45 C.F.R. § 205.50.
49. G.S. 7B-302(a1)(1). This mandate may not apply to disclosure of the identity of the reporter. See the discussion above.

other parties that do not involve child welfare."[50] (See further discussion of private civil cases, below.)

DSS has discretion in determining which information it should provide to the government entity pursuant to this provision. The agency will need to evaluate the request and determine which information is necessary to protect the child from abuse or neglect. DSS must not disclose information pursuant to this provision if it is subject to other, more stringent confidentiality laws, such as the federal substance abuse confidentiality regulations.[51]

Once information is disclosed pursuant to G.S. 7B-302, it remains confidential and may be re-disclosed only "for purposes directly connected with carrying out that entity's mandated responsibilities." Therefore, if DSS elects to make a disclosure to a government entity in order to protect the juvenile, it should make a deliberate effort to inform the entity receiving the information that it has a duty to keep the information confidential consistent with the recipient's own legal duties.

Sharing with Designated Agencies

As mentioned above, G.S. 7B-3100 and the accompanying regulations require designated agencies to share information for the purpose of protecting the child (and also for educational purposes). The agencies authorized by regulation to share information include

- the Department of Juvenile Justice and Delinquency Prevention;[52]
- the Office of the Guardian Ad Litem Services of the Administrative Office of the Courts;
- county departments of social services;
- area mental health, developmental disability, and substance abuse authorities;
- local law enforcement agencies;

---

50. NC Division of Social Services, Family Services Manual, Vol. I, Ch. VIII, Sec. 1426, Change # 06-2008, at 4 (July 2008), http://info.dhhs.state.nc.us/olm/manuals/dss/csm-60/man/pdf%20docs/CS1428.pdf.

51. *Id*. See also the discussion in Chapter 5 regarding the federal substance abuse regulations.

52. In 2012, the Department of Juvenile Justice and Delinquency Prevention was integrated into the Department of Public Safety (DPS). DPS now includes a Juvenile Justice Section in the Division of Adult and Juvenile Correction. See www.ncdps.gov/index2.cfm?a=000003,002476.

- district attorneys' offices, as authorized by 7B-3100;[53]
- county mental health facilities and developmental disabilities and substance abuse programs;[54]
- local school administrative units; and
- local health departments.

In addition, the regulations allow a chief district court judge to issue an administrative order identifying other agencies as "designated agencies."[55] Administrative orders vary in the level of detail they offer and the types of agencies identified. Some identify only public agencies and officials, repeating many that are identified in the statute and regulations. Others take a more expansive view of the term "agency" and include some private entities, such as community health centers, hospitals, youth centers, and counseling programs. The terms "agency" and "local agency" are not defined in the statute or regulations, so it is conceivable that the law was intended to encompass both public and private entities.

The statute requires sharing if it is relevant to

- any assessment of a report of child abuse, neglect, or dependency;
- the provision or arrangement of protective services in a child abuse, neglect, or dependency case by DSS; or
- any case in which a petition is filed alleging that a juvenile is abused, neglected, dependent, undisciplined, or delinquent.

The statute applies to information sharing both before and after a petition is filed. Prior to 2006, the statute was limited to cases in which a petition had been filed. It was amended at that point to include assessments and the arrangement for and provision of protective services.[56] The applicable

---

53. G.S. 7B-3100 provides that the information sharing with the district attorney only goes in one direction—from DSS to the district attorney. "Nothing herein shall be deemed to require the disclosure or release of any information in the possession of the district attorney." G.S. 7B-3100(a).

54. This regulation uses outdated terminology to refer to the public system for providing mental health, developmental disability, and substance abuse services. *See* Mark Botts, *Mental Health Services*, *in* County and Municipal Government in North Carolina 698–702 (Frayda S. Bluestein ed., UNC School of Government, 2015).

55. 14B NCAC 11A .0301. The judge has authority to issue orders applicable to agencies within the judge's district.

56. S.L. 2006-250, sec. 2.

state regulation, however, has not been updated to reflect the full scope of authority granted by the revised statute so it limits information sharing to only those cases in which a petition has been filed.[57] As a result, there is a disconnect between the statute and the regulations. DSS should rely on the statute.

Disclosing Pursuant to a Court Order

After a petition has been filed in juvenile court, G.S. 7B-2901(c) allows a court to order public agencies to share information "as the court deems necessary to reduce the trauma" to a child victim.[58] This type of disclosure obviously requires the court to take an affirmative step to order agencies to share, and therefore it may be seen as cumbersome at times.

Disclosing to Law Enforcement Officials

Upon receiving a report, DSS is required to share information with the district attorney and law enforcement officials if it

- finds evidence that a child may have been abused by a parent, guardian, custodian, or caretaker, or
- receives information that a child may have been physically harmed in violation of a criminal law by a person who is not the child's parent, guardian, custodian, or caretaker.[59]

DSS has a very limited amount of time to make this contact. It must submit an oral report, followed by a written report, within forty-eight hours of receiving the information.[60] At this stage, DSS is expressly authorized to disclose the information it gathered from the reporter about the child, the child's family, the alleged perpetrator, the injury or condition, and any other information that may be helpful. Also, as mentioned above, DSS is allowed

---

57. 14B NCAC 11A .0301.

58. G.S. 7B-2901(c).

59. G.S. 7B-307(a); 10A NCAC 70A .0105. These types of cases are beyond the scope of DSS's authority and the agency will not be able to provide protective services to the child.

60. G.S. 7B-307(a); 10A NCAC 70A .0105(c). *See also* NC DIVISION OF SOCIAL SERVICES, FAMILY SERVICES MANUAL, Vol. 1, Ch. VIII, Sec. 1407, at 6–7 (June 2008), http://info.dhhs.state.nc.us/olm/manuals/dss/csm-60/man/pdf%20docs/CS1407.pdf.

to share the identity of the reporter "when necessary for law enforcement to perform their duties. . . ."[61]

Beyond this mandatory reporting, other laws also authorize DSS to share information with law enforcement if the disclosure is for the purpose of protecting a child. As discussed above, G.S. 7B-302 requires DSS to disclose information to government officials in order to *protect a child* from abuse or neglect.[62] G.S. 7B-3100 has similar language in that it allows disclosure to designated agencies (including law enforcement officials) if the information will be used, more generally, for the protection of the child or others.

There are certainly circumstances where DSS will conclude that disclosure to law enforcement officials is necessary to protect a child. In those instances, DSS *must* disclose the information. Note that both statutes cast wide nets for protection; they are not limited in scope to disclosures necessary to protect only the child who is the subject of the report or assessment. Therefore, if sharing CPS information with law enforcement officials would help them protect *any* child, DSS must disclose the information.

Other laws require DSS to share information with governmental agencies in specific circumstances. See "Mandatory Reporting and Notification," below, for more details.

To the Juvenile's Guardian ad Litem

After a petition is filed, the court may appoint a guardian ad litem (GAL) to represent the juvenile.[63] Once appointed, the GAL has expansive authority to obtain information from DSS and from others as well. The statute provides that the GAL

> [h]as the authority to obtain any information or reports, whether or not confidential, that may in the guardian ad litem's opinion be

---

61. 10A NCAC 70A .0105(c).

62. G.S. 7B-302(a1)(1). The regulation implementing G.S. 7B-302 authorizes disclosure to the district attorney or his designee information "which he needs to carry out his mandated responsibilities that result from a report of confirmed abuse." 10A NCAC 70A .0113. Because the regulation is based on the authority in G.S. 7B-302 and it cannot exceed the scope of statute, it is reasonable to infer that the regulation also requires DSS to determine that such a disclosure is "necessary to protect a juvenile from abuse or neglect."

63. G.S. 7B-601(a). The court is required to appoint a guardian ad litem (GAL) if the petition alleges abuse or neglect. The court is allowed (but not required) to appoint a GAL if the petition alleges dependency.

relevant to the case. No privilege other than the attorney–client privilege may be invoked to prevent the guardian ad litem and the court from obtaining such information.[64]

The law further requires that the GAL keep the information confidential, disclosing it only if ordered to do so by a court or "otherwise provided by law."[65]

Note that even though this provision grants the GAL expansive access to records, this authority does not extend to information protected by the federal substance abuse confidentiality regulations.[66] See Chapter 5. DSS should not disclose any such information to the GAL without a court order that complies with those federal regulations.

Interestingly, language in both G.S. 7B-302 and G.S. 7B-2901 grants a child and the child's guardian ad litem a right to "examine" confidential information (see the discussion of the child's right of access in Chapter 6). Similarly, 10A NCAC 70A .0113 grants the child's attorney the right to examine DSS's protective services case record.[67] This additional right of access for the GAL seems superfluous, however, given the expansive authority to obtain information granted to the GAL in other laws.

To Collateral Sources

Upon receiving a report, DSS is required by law to gather information about the child and the situation. In the course of gathering information, DSS will need to contact "collateral sources"—that is, other people or organizations that may have relevant information, such as schools, medical providers, and out-of-home care providers. DSS is authorized to contact them for information but is required to "exercise discretion in the selection of collateral sources in order to protect the family's or out-of-home care setting's right to

---

64. G.S. 7B-601(c). *See In re* N.C.L., 89 N.C. App. 79, *cert. denied*, 322 N.C. 481 (1988) (authorizing disclosure of confidential adoption records to guardian ad litem); Wilkinson v. Riffel, 72 N.C. App. 220 (1984) (same).

65. G.S. 7B-601(c). *See also* G.S. 7B-700(f) ("Unless provided otherwise by local rules, information or reports obtained by the guardian ad litem pursuant to G.S. 7B-601 are not subject to disclosure pursuant to [a discovery request], except that reports and records shall be shared with all parties before submission to the court.).

66. 42 C.F.R. Part 2.

67. *See* 10A NCAC 70A .0112 (specifying the information to be included in the protective services case record).

privacy and the confidentiality of the report."[68] This guidance implies that DSS may need to share very limited information with a collateral source in the process of conducting an assessment.

In a Private Civil Case

Parties to a civil case, such as a divorce or child custody matter that does not involve DSS, may want to present evidence that is derived from DSS records of a child protective services case. A district or superior court judge presiding over the case may order DSS to release confidential information, but it must (1) provide DSS with notice and an opportunity to be heard, (2) determine that the information is relevant and necessary to the civil case, and (3) determine that the information is unavailable from any other source.[69] DSS may want to ask the judge to conduct an *in camera* review of the records before ordering the release.

One could argue that because a parent or guardian has a right to obtain a copy of the DSS record about his or her child, it is unnecessary for a parent or guardian who is a party in a civil case to seek a court order. In other words, the parent or guardian should simply be able to request a copy of the record from DSS. The question of parental right of access is complex and is discussed in more detail in Chapter 6.

To a Child or Adult Who Is Involved in a Criminal or Delinquency Case

There are two different types of requests that could fall into this category:

- requests from the person who is the subject of the CPS case, while that person is still a child, is an adult, or has been emancipated;
- requests from a person who is not the subject of the CPS case, such as a parent, caretaker, or sibling of a child who is the subject.

---

68. 10A NCAC 70A .0106(i) and (j).

69. G.S. 7B-302(a1)(3). *See* Ritter v. Kimball, 67 N.C. App. 333 (1984) (upholding lower court's decision to order DSS to disclose confidential DSS records in a civil custody case, with the exception of the identity of the reporter and information that may be used to identify the reporter). *See also* Brunson v. N.C. Dep't of Soc. Servs., 2013 WL 1768681 (E.D.N.C. Apr. 24, 2013) *reconsideration denied in part*, 2013 WL 3923996 (E.D.N.C. July 29, 2013) (unreported; authorizing discovery of confidential DSS records in civil case, issuing a protective order, and requiring *in camera* review).

The first type of request is discussed in Chapter 6 because it is connected to the child's right of access.

The second type of request is fairly common and has been addressed by both the courts and the legislature. In summary, the US Supreme Court held that a defendant in a criminal proceeding has a constitutional right to have access to information held by third parties if that information is favorable and material to his or her defense.[70] In 2009, the state legislature amended the state laws governing confidentiality of CPS records to provide that

> [a] district or superior court judge of this State presiding over a criminal or delinquency matter shall conduct an in camera review prior to releasing to the defendant or juvenile any confidential records maintained by the department of social services, except those records the defendant or juvenile is entitled to pursuant to subdivision (2) of this subsection.[71]

Therefore, if DSS receives a subpoena or a court order for disclosure of CPS records in a criminal case or delinquency adjudication, DSS should ask the court to conduct an *in camera* review of the records before ordering the agency to release them to the defendant.[72]

From the Central Registry

The state maintains a registry of abuse, neglect, and dependency cases. The state uses the registry to collect centralized information so that it can be shared quickly with counties and other states if necessary to protect a child.

---

70. G.S. 7B-302(a1)(4); G.S. 7B-2901(b)(3). This language codifies the defendants' constitutional right to confidential records maintained by a third party. *See* Pennsylvania v. Ritchie, 480 U.S. 39 (1987); State v. McGill, 141 N.C. App 98, 101 (2000). *See also* John Rubin, NC DEFENDER MANUAL, Vol. 1, Pretrial, Sec. 4.6 (UNC School of Government, 2d ed. 2013), http://defendermanuals.sog.unc.edu/; Jessica Smith, *Defendant's Right to Third Party Confidential Records*, NORTH CAROLINA CRIMINAL LAW BLOG (Oct. 2, 2014), http://nccriminallaw.sog.unc.edu/defendants-right-to-third-party-confidential-records/.

71. G.S. 7B-302(a1)(4); G.S. 7B 2901(b)(3).

72. *See also* JOHN RUBIN, NC DEFENDER MANUAL, Vol. 1, Pretrial, Sec. 4.6 (UNC School of Government, 2d ed. 2013), http://defendermanuals.sog.unc.edu/ (suggesting that the attorney for the defendant or the juvenile may ask that the court recognize him or her as an officer of the court and allow the attorney to review the records to identify those that are material and favorable).

Identifiable information in the registry is confidential, and there are strict limitations on access to and use of the information.[73]

DSS may access the registry in order to identify whether a child has been previously reported as abused or neglected or whether the child is part of a family that experienced a child fatality due to suspected abuse or neglect. It may share information from the registry with law enforcement officials, licensed physicians, or physician extenders "when needed to assist . . . in facilitating the provision of child protective services . . . ."[74] DSS may share the following limited information from the registry:

- the child's name, date of birth, sex, and race;
- the county that investigated the report;
- the type of maltreatment that was reported;
- the case decision and the date of that decision;
- the type of maltreatment found; and
- the relationship of the perpetrator to the victim.

A DSS staff member may be charged with a Class 3 misdemeanor if he or she knowingly and willfully releases information from the central registry to a person who is not authorized to receive it.[75]

If DSS is sharing information with another government agency, either in or out of state, and it is doing so for the purpose of protecting a child from abuse or neglect, DSS would not need to draw on the central registry for information or comply with the limitations on the types of information to be disclosed. As discussed earlier in this chapter, G.S. 7B-302 provides expansive authority for DSS to disclose information to government officials for that purpose. In addition, 10A NCAC 70A .0113 allows sharing information with "public or private agencies or individuals that are being utilized to provide or facilitate the provision of protective services to a child."[76]

_____

73. G.S. 7B-311; 10A NCAC 70A .0102.
74. 10A NCAC 70A .0102(b)(3).
75. G.S. 7B-311(c).
76. While the state regulation, 70A NCAC .0113, allows disclosures to private agencies and individuals, the statutes cited as authority for the regulations are not quite as broad. G.S. 7B-302 allows disclosure to a "federal, State, or local government entity _or its agent_" (emphasis added) if disclosure is for the purpose of protecting the child. If a private entity or individual is an agent of the government entity, disclosure would be permitted. If it is not an agent, it is unclear whether this state regulation provides sufficient authority to disclose.

Mandatory Notification and Information Sharing

In several situations, DSS is required to disclose information that would otherwise be considered confidential. Because it is required by state law, DSS may make these disclosures without violating applicable state confidentiality laws. If, however, the information is protected by another law, such as the federal substance abuse confidentiality regulation, DSS may not be able to disclose it or may need to take steps to redact some of the information in order to comply with the other law.

Below are brief summaries of some of these mandatory disclosures. Note that this list may not be exhaustive; there may be other state or federal laws that could be interpreted to require disclosure.

Upon Receiving a Report

When DSS receives a report indicating that a child may be in need of protective services, it is required to make several specific types of disclosures:

- *Report to law enforcement.* As discussed above, DSS is required to share information with the district attorney and law enforcement officials immediately after receiving a report if there is evidence that a child may have been (1) abused by a parent, guardian, custodian, or caretaker or (2) physically harmed by a person other than a parent, guardian, custodian, or caretaker and the harm appears to be in violation of a criminal law.[77]
- *Report involving a child care facility.* If DSS receives a report that involves abuse, neglect, or maltreatment[78] of a child who is in child care, the agency must notify the North Carolina Department of Health and Human Services (NC DHHS) within twenty-four hours of receiving the report or on the next working day.[79]
- *Report involving a child from another county.* If DSS determines that the child's legal residence is in another county, it must promptly

---

77. G.S. 7B-307(a); 10A NCAC 70A .0105(c).

78. The term "maltreatment" has a specific meaning in the context of child care facilities. It is defined, in part, as "any act or series of acts of commission or omission by a caregiver that results in harm, potential for harm, or threat of harm to a child." G.S. 110-105.3(b)(3) (added by S.L. 2015-123).

79. G.S. 7B-307(a).

notify the other county and the two agencies must coordinate efforts.[80]

- *Report involving a child in another state.* If DSS receives a report that involves abuse or neglect of a child in another state, guidance issued by the state directs DSS to communicate that report to the appropriate CPS agency in the other state.[81]
- *Report involving a child in an institution.* If DSS receives a report that abuse, neglect, or dependency occurred in an institution, it must notify the person who is administratively responsible for the institution.[82]
- *In a case involving a missing child.* If DSS receives a report alleging abandonment, DSS must ask law enforcement officials to investigate whether the juvenile is a missing child.[83]

When the Assessment Reveals the Presence of Abuse, Neglect, or Dependency

DSS is required to make several types of disclosures if an assessment reveals that a child has been abused or neglected or is dependent:

- *In all cases.* DSS is required to submit information about the case to the central registry.[84]
- *In all cases.* DSS is required to "make every effort to provide personal written notice" of the finding to the following:
  - any responsible individual[85] who is alleged to have abused or seriously neglected the child,[86]
  - any parent or other individual with whom the child resided at the time the investigation was initiated,[87]

---

80. G.S. 7B-302(a2).

81. NC Division of Social Services, Family Services Manual, Vol. I, Ch. VIII, Sec. 1407, at 7 (Jan. 2007), http://info.dhhs.state.nc.us/olm/manuals/dss/csm-60/man/pdf%20docs/CS1407.pdf.

82. 10A NCAC 70A .0105(f).

83. G.S. 7B-302(a).

84. G.S. 7B-307(c).

85. The term "responsible individual" is defined as a "parent, guardian, custo-dian, or caretaker who abuses or seriously neglects a juvenile." *See* G.S. 7B-101(18a).

86. 10A NCAC 70A .0107(a).

87. *Id.*

- any agency that has legal custody of the child,[88] and
- the person who made the report (see "Notifying the Reporter," below).

- *In a case involving a child in an institution.* If the report is ultimately confirmed, DSS is required to notify the child's legal custodian and the district attorney in the county where the institution is located.[89]

When the Assessment Does Not Reveal the Presence of Abuse, Neglect, or Dependency

If DSS does not conclude that abuse, neglect, or dependency is present, the agency must notify the following people of the case findings:

- any parent or caretaker who was alleged to have abused or neglected the child or children,
- any parent or other person with whom the child or children resided at the time DSS initiated the investigation,
- any agency that has legal custody of the child or children,[90] and
- the person who made the report.

Notifying the Reporter

The person who submitted the initial CPS report is entitled to two types of notice from DSS. First, within five working days of receiving the report, DSS must provide the reporter with written notice explaining whether the report was accepted by DSS for protective services assessment or whether it was referred to law enforcement officials.[91] Second, within five working days after completing the assessment, DSS must provide the reporter with written notice explaining the case finding, what action will be taken next, and, if DSS has decided not to file a petition in the case, the process for requesting that the district attorney review that decision.[92] While the reporter is entitled to receive these two types of written notice, the reporter may prefer to remain anonymous or may ask DSS not to provide either or both notices.[93]

---

88. *Id.*
89. 10A NCAC 70A .0107(f).
90. 10A NCAC 70A .0108.
91. G.S. 7B-302(f); 10A NCAC 70A .0109(a).
92. G.S. 7B-302(g); 10A NCAC 70A .0109.
93. Some reports are anonymous.

If the reporter asks the district attorney to review the case and the district attorney sends DSS written notice regarding the review, DSS must send a copy of the investigation report to the district attorney within three working days.[94]

Sharing Information with Foster Parents

Federal law requires DSS to compile a case plan that includes certain information about the child's health and education, including

- the names and addresses of the child's health and educational providers,
- the child's grade level performance,
- the child's school record,
- the child's immunizations,
- the child's known medical problems, and
- the child's medications.[95]

DSS must provide this information to the foster family along with "any other relevant health and education information concerning the child determined to be appropriate by the State agency."[96]

In addition, a state regulation provides that DSS must "include foster parents as part of the decision-making team for a child," which necessarily implies that the agency will share information with the foster parents. The state regulation is not as specific as the federal law, however.[97]

---

94. 10A NCAC 70A .0109(b).

95. 42 U.S.C. § 671 (a)(16) (requiring a case plan); 42 U.S.C. § 675(1)(C) (health and education records that must be included in case plan); 42 U.S.C. § 675(5)(D) (requiring that the health and education information be shared with foster families). *See also* 45 C.F.R. §§ 1356.21(f) and (h) (detailing requirements for the case plan and case plan review).

96. 42 U.S.C. § 675(5)(D).

97. 10A NCAC 70 .0903.

Reporting Child Fatalities and Near Fatalities

All child fatalities must be reported to the central registry, which is maintained by the state.[98] In addition, if a child dies or almost dies as a result of suspected abuse, neglect, or maltreatment,[99] the public is entitled to have access to a written summary of certain information from the records of any public agency, including DSS, if the following two conditions are satisfied:

- *Information must be requested.* A member of the public must request the information. DSS is not required to release the information or otherwise make it publicly available without a request.
- *Information must be connected to a crime.* There must be some amount of potential criminal liability involved with the case. Either (1) a person must be criminally charged with having caused the fatality or near fatality, or (2) the district attorney must certify that a person who is dead would have been criminally charged had that person still been alive.

If these two conditions are satisfied, DSS may disclose a written summary "of actions taken or services rendered by a public agency following receipt of information that a child might be in need of protection."[100] The law provides examples of the types of information that may be included and explains that agencies are not required to disclose (1) information that would reveal the identity of the reporter or other individuals who provided information or (2) "the substance or content of any psychiatric, psychological, or therapeutic evaluations . . . pertaining to the child or the child's family unless directly related to the cause of the child fatality or near fatality."

---

98. G.S. 7B-307(c).

99. This law applies to child fatalities and near fatalities. A "child fatality" is "the death of a child from suspected abuse, neglect, or maltreatment." A "near fatality" is "a case in which a physician determines that a child is in serious or critical condition as the result of sickness or injury caused by suspected abuse, neglect, or maltreatment." G.S. 7B-2902(a).

100. G.S. 7B-2902(a)(2) (definition of findings and information). *See also* 42 U.S.C. § 5106(b)(2)(x) (CAPTA provision authorizing public disclosure in child fatality cases).

In some circumstances, the agency is allowed to deny this type of request, but before doing so it must first consult with the district attorney.[101] A person whose request has been denied may ask a superior court judge to review the decision and may further appeal that decision as well.

State, Federal, and Local Oversight

Some laws require or allow DSS to share identifiable information with state and federal agencies involved in oversight of the CPS program. For example:

- DSS is allowed to share information with the NC DHHS for the purposes of supervision and reporting.[102]
- The local and State Child Fatality Prevention Teams are allowed to have access to confidential DSS records in the course of conducting reviews of child fatalities.

Such disclosures are permitted by state and federal law because they are "directly connected with the administration" of the CPS program.[103]

In addition to state and federal oversight, each DSS has a governing board. In most counties, it is an appointed county board of social services or a consolidated human services board.[104] In some counties, the board of county commissioners has abolished the appointed governing board and assumed its powers and duties.[105] The board plays an oversight role with the agency. Depending on the type of board a county has in place, it may hire and supervise the director of social services,[106] consult with the direc-

---

101. An agency may deny a request if it has a reasonable belief that disclosure (1) is not authorized by state or federal law, (2) is likely to cause harm or danger to a minor child living in the deceased or injured child's household, (3) is likely to jeopardize the state's ability to prosecute the defendant, (4) is likely to jeopardize the defendant's right to a fair trial, or (5) is likely to undermine an ongoing or future criminal investigation. G.S. 7B-2902(d).

102. 10A NCAC 69 .0501.

103. G.S. 108A-80; 10A NCAC 69 .0501(b)(4) (disclosures permitted "for purposes of supervision and reporting); 10A NCAC 70A .0113 (authorizing disclosure to "state and federal agency personnel carrying out their lawful responsibilities for program audit and review").

104. G.S. 108A-1.

105. G.S. 153A-77(a).

106. In a consolidated human services agency, the relationship between the governing board and the director is different. The county manager hires and dismisses

tor about problems, assist the director with the budget, and advise county officials on "social conditions of the county."[107] It also plays a role in fraud investigations.[108]

As discussed in Chapter 2, there is some question about whether DSS board members are entitled to have access to identifiable CPS information in the context of program oversight. G.S. 108A-109 allows members of county boards of social services or consolidated human services boards to "inspect and examine any record on file in the office of the director relating in any manner to applications for and provision of public assistance and social services . . . ."[109]

It is conceivable that a board or board member would want to have access to CPS information in the course of exercising oversight authority. There is a confusing advisory opinion from the North Carolina Attorney General's office that takes the position that the state's CPS-specific confidentiality laws prohibit DSS from sharing CPS records with the governing board pursuant to G.S .108A-9.[110] The opinion goes on, however, to state that "DSS directors may in their discretion bring individual juvenile records before the social services board for their review." It is difficult to reconcile these two conflicting conclusions and understand the scope of the board members' right of access.

This opinion was based on an older, now repealed, version of the state confidentiality law,[111] but the general tone of the confidentiality protections remains the same or is perhaps even more stringent now. Given the existence of this opinion and the strong language in G.S. 7B-302 requiring that CPS information be held in the "strictest confidence," the most cautious approach DSS could take would be to prohibit sharing of identifiable

---

the director with the advice and consent of the consolidated human services board. G.S. 153A-77(e).

107. G.S. 108A-9.

108. *See* Aimee Wall, *Boards of Social Services and Fraud Investigations,* Coates' Canons: NC Local Government Law Blog (Apr. 18, 2012), http://canons.sog.unc.edu/?p=6603.

109. G.S. 108A-11.

110. North Carolina Department of Justice, Advisory Opinion: Access to Records by Social Services Boards, Letter to Kevin M. Fitzgerald, Director of the Division of Social Services (Apr. 20, 1995).

111. G.S. 7A-675 (repealed effective July 1, 1999).

CPS-related information with the agency's governing board. If it does allow the board to have access, the agency should ensure that board members understand that the information is confidential and must not be further disclosed.[112] An intermediate option could be to provide board members with access to de-identified information.

112. G.S. 108A-9.

Relevant Statutes
North Carolina General Statutes

§ 7B-302. Assessment by director; access to confidential information; notification of person making the report.

(a) When a report of abuse, neglect, or dependency is received, the director of the department of social services shall make a prompt and thorough assessment, using either a family assessment response or an investigative assessment response, in order to ascertain the facts of the case, the extent of the abuse or neglect, and the risk of harm to the juvenile, in order to determine whether protective services should be provided or the complaint filed as a petition. When the report alleges abuse, the director shall immediately, but no later than 24 hours after receipt of the report, initiate the assessment. When the report alleges neglect or dependency, the director shall initiate the assessment within 72 hours following receipt of the report. When the report alleges abandonment, the director shall immediately initiate an assessment, take appropriate steps to assume temporary custody of the juvenile, and take appropriate steps to secure an order for nonsecure custody of the juvenile. The assessment and evaluation shall include a visit to the place where the juvenile resides, except when the report alleges abuse or neglect in a child care facility as defined in Article 7 of Chapter 110 of the General Statutes. When a report alleges abuse or neglect in a child care facility as defined in Article 7 of Chapter 110 of the General Statutes, a visit to the place where the juvenile resides is not required. When the report alleges abandonment, the assessment shall include a request from the director to law enforcement officials to investigate through the North Carolina Center for Missing Persons and other national and State resources whether the juvenile is a missing child.

(a1) All information received by the department of social services, including the identity of the reporter, shall be held in strictest confidence by the department, except under the following circumstances:

(1) The department shall disclose confidential information to any federal, State, or local government entity or its agent in order to protect a juvenile from abuse or neglect. Any confidential information disclosed to any federal, State, or local government entity or its agent under this subsection shall remain confidential with the other government entity or its agent and shall only be redisclosed for purposes directly connected with carrying out that entity's mandated responsibilities.

(1a) The department shall disclose confidential information regarding the identity of the reporter to any federal, State, or local government entity or its agent with a court order. The department may only disclose confidential information regarding the identity of the reporter to a federal, State, or local government entity or its agent without a court order when the entity demonstrates a need for the reporter's name to carry out the entity's mandated responsibilities.

(2)   The information may be examined upon request by the juvenile's guardian ad litem or the juvenile, including a juvenile who has reached age 18 or been emancipated.

(3)   A district or superior court judge of this State presiding over a civil matter in which the department of social services is not a party may order the department to release confidential information, after providing the department with reasonable notice and an opportunity to be heard and then determining that the information is relevant and necessary to the trial of the matter before the court and unavailable from any other source. This subdivision shall not be construed to relieve any court of its duty to conduct hearings and make findings required under relevant federal law, before ordering the release of any private medical or mental health information or records related to substance abuse or HIV status or treatment. The department of social services may surrender the requested records to the court, for in camera review, if the surrender is necessary to make the required determinations.

(4)   A district or superior court judge of this State presiding over a criminal or delinquency matter shall conduct an in camera review prior to releasing to the defendant or juvenile any confidential records maintained by the department of social services, except those records the defendant or juvenile is entitled to pursuant to subdivision (2) of this subsection.

(5)   The department may disclose confidential information to a parent, guardian, custodian, or caretaker in accordance with G.S. 7B700 of this Subchapter.

(a2) If the director, at any time after receiving a report that a juvenile may be abused, neglected, or dependent, determines that the juvenile's legal residence is in another county, the director shall promptly notify the director in the county of the juvenile's residence, and the two directors shall coordinate efforts to ensure that appropriate actions are taken.

(b) When a report of a juvenile's death as a result of suspected maltreatment or a report of suspected abuse, neglect, or dependency of a juvenile in a noninstitutional setting is received, the director of the department of social services shall immediately ascertain if other juveniles live in the home, and, if so, initiate an assessment in order to determine whether they require protective services or whether immediate removal of the juveniles from the home is necessary for their protection. When a report of a juvenile's death as a result of maltreatment or a report of suspected abuse, neglect, or dependency of a juvenile in an institutional setting such as a residential child care facility or residential educational facility is received, the director of the department of social services shall immediately ascertain if other juveniles remain in the facility subject to the alleged perpetrator's care or supervision, and, if so, assess the circumstances of those juveniles in order to determine whether they require protective services or whether immediate removal of those juveniles from the facility is necessary for their protection.

(c) If the assessment indicates that abuse, neglect, or dependency has occurred, the director shall decide whether immediate removal of the juvenile or any other juveniles in the home is necessary for their protection. If immediate removal does not seem necessary, the director shall immediately provide or arrange for protective services. If the parent, guardian, custodian, or caretaker refuses to accept the protective services provided or arranged by the director, the director shall sign a petition seeking to invoke the jurisdiction of the court for the protection of the juvenile or juveniles.

(d) If immediate removal seems necessary for the protection of the juvenile or other juveniles in the home, the director shall sign a petition that alleges the applicable facts to invoke the jurisdiction of the court. Where the assessment shows that it is warranted, a protective services worker may assume temporary custody of the juvenile for the juvenile's protection pursuant to Article 5 of this Chapter.

(d1) Whenever a juvenile is removed from the home of a parent, guardian, custodian, stepparent, or adult relative entrusted with the juvenile's care due to physical abuse, the director shall conduct a thorough review of the background of the alleged abuser or abusers. This review shall include a criminal history check and a review of any available mental health records. If the review reveals that the alleged abuser or abusers have a history of violent behavior against people, the director shall petition the court to order the alleged abuser or abusers to submit to a complete mental health evaluation by a licensed psychologist or psychiatrist.

(e) In performing any duties related to the assessment of the report or the provision or arrangement for protective services, the director may consult with any public or private agencies or individuals, including the available State or local law enforcement officers who shall assist in the assessment and evaluation of the seriousness of any report of abuse, neglect, or dependency when requested by the director. The director or the director's representative may make a written demand for any information or reports, whether or not confidential, that may in the director's opinion be relevant to the assessment or provision of protective services. Upon the director's or the director's representative's request and unless protected by the attorney-client privilege, any public or private agency or individual shall provide access to and copies of this confidential information and these records to the extent permitted by federal law and regulations. If a custodian of criminal investigative information or records believes that release of the information will jeopardize the right of the State to prosecute a defendant or the right of a defendant to receive a fair trial or will undermine an ongoing or future investigation, it may seek an order from a court of competent jurisdiction to prevent disclosure of the information. In such an action, the custodian of the records shall have the burden of showing by a preponderance of the evidence that disclosure of the information in question will jeopardize the right of the State to prosecute a defendant or the right of a defendant to receive a fair trial or will undermine an ongoing or future investigation. Actions brought pursuant to this paragraph shall be set down for immediate hearing, and subsequent proceedings in the actions shall be accorded priority by the trial and appellate courts.

(f) Within five working days after receipt of the report of abuse, neglect, or dependency, the director shall give written notice to the person making the report, unless requested by that person not to give notice, as to whether the report was accepted for assessment and whether the report was referred to the appropriate State or local law enforcement agency.

(g) Within five working days after completion of the protective services assessment, the director shall give subsequent written notice to the person making the report, unless requested by that person not to give notice, as to whether there is a finding of abuse, neglect, or dependency, whether the county department of social services is taking action to protect the juvenile, and what action it is taking, including whether or not a petition was filed. The person making the report shall be informed of procedures necessary to request a review by the prosecutor of the director's decision not to file a petition. A request for review by the prosecutor shall be made within five working days of receipt of the second notification. The second notification shall include notice that, if the person making the report is not satisfied with the director's decision, the person may request review of the decision by the prosecutor within five working days of receipt. The person making the report may waive the person's right to this notification, and no notification is required if the person making the report does not identify himself to the director.

(h) The director or the director's representative may not enter a private residence for assessment purposes without at least one of the following:

(1) The reasonable belief that a juvenile is in imminent danger of death or serious physical injury.
(2) The permission of the parent or person responsible for the juvenile's care.
(3) The accompaniment of a law enforcement officer who has legal authority to enter the residence.
(4) An order from a court of competent jurisdiction.

§ 7B-2901. Confidentiality of records.

(a) The clerk shall maintain a complete record of all juvenile cases filed in the clerk's office alleging abuse, neglect, or dependency. The records shall be withheld from public inspection and, except as provided in this subsection, may be examined only by order of the court. The record shall include the summons, petition, custody order, court order, written motions, the electronic or mechanical recording of the hearing, and other papers filed in the proceeding. The recording of the hearing shall be reduced to a written transcript only when notice of appeal has been timely given. After the time for appeal has expired with no appeal having been filed, the recording of the hearing may be erased or destroyed upon the written order of the court.

The following persons may examine the juvenile's record maintained pursuant to this subsection and obtain copies of written parts of the record without an order of the court:

(1) The person named in the petition as the juvenile;
(2) The guardian ad litem;

(3) The county department of social services; and

(4) The juvenile's parent, guardian, or custodian, or the attorney for the juvenile or the juvenile's parent, guardian, or custodian.

(b) The Director of the Department of Social Services shall maintain a record of the cases of juveniles under protective custody by the Department or under placement by the court, which shall include family background information; reports of social, medical, psychiatric, or psychological information concerning a juvenile or the juvenile's family; interviews with the juvenile's family; or other information which the court finds should be protected from public inspection in the best interests of the juvenile. The records maintained pursuant to this subsection may be examined only in the following circumstances:

(1) The juvenile's guardian ad litem or the juvenile, including a juvenile who has reached age 18 or been emancipated, may examine the records.

(2) A district or superior court judge of this State presiding over a civil matter in which the department is not a party may order the department to release confidential information, after providing the department with reasonable notice and an opportunity to be heard and then determining that the information is relevant and necessary to the trial of the matter before the court and unavailable from any other source. This subsection shall not be construed to relieve any court of its duty to conduct hearings and make findings required under relevant federal law before ordering the release of any private medical or mental health information or records related to substance abuse or HIV status or treatment. The department may surrender the requested records to the court, for in camera review, if surrender is necessary to make the required determinations.

(3) A district or superior court judge of this State presiding over a criminal or delinquency matter shall conduct an in camera review before releasing to the defendant or juvenile any confidential records maintained by the department of social services, except those records the defendant or juvenile is entitled to pursuant to subdivision (1) of this subsection.

(4) The department may disclose confidential information to a parent, guardian, custodian, or caretaker in accordance with G.S. 7B700.

(c) In the case of a child victim, the court may order the sharing of information among such public agencies as the court deems necessary to reduce the trauma to the victim.

(d) The court's entire record of a proceeding involving consent for an abortion on an unemancipated minor under Article 1A, Part 2 of Chapter 90 of the General Statutes is not a matter of public record, shall be maintained separately from any juvenile record, shall be withheld from public inspection, and may be examined only by order of the court, by the unemancipated minor, or by the unemancipated minor's attorney or guardian ad litem.

§ 7B-3100. Disclosure of information about juveniles.

(a) The Division, after consultation with the Conference of Chief District Court Judges, shall adopt rules designating certain local agencies that are authorized to share information concerning juveniles in accordance with the provisions of this section. Agencies so designated shall share with one another, upon request and to the extent permitted by federal law and regulations, information that is in their possession that is relevant to any assessment of a report of child abuse, neglect, or dependency or the provision or arrangement of protective services in a child abuse, neglect, or dependency case by a local department of social services pursuant to the authority granted under Chapter 7B of the General Statutes or to any case in which a petition is filed alleging that a juvenile is abused, neglected, dependent, undisciplined, or delinquent and shall continue to do so until the protective services case is closed by the local department of social services, or if a petition is filed when the juvenile is no longer subject to the jurisdiction of juvenile court. Agencies that may be designated as "agencies authorized to share information" include local mental health facilities, local health departments, local departments of social services, local law enforcement agencies, local school administrative units, the district's district attorney's office, the Division of Juvenile Justice of the Department of Public Safety, and the Office of Guardian ad Litem Services of the Administrative Office of the Courts, and, pursuant to the provisions of G.S. 7B3000(e1), the Section of Community Corrections of the Division of Adult Correction of the Department of Public Safety. Any information shared among agencies pursuant to this section shall remain confidential, shall be withheld from public inspection, and shall be used only for the protection of the juvenile and others or to improve the educational opportunities of the juvenile, and shall be released in accordance with the provisions of the Family Educational and Privacy Rights Act as set forth in 20 U.S.C. § 1232g. Nothing in this section or any other provision of law shall preclude any other necessary sharing of information among agencies. Nothing herein shall be deemed to require the disclosure or release of any information in the possession of a district attorney.

(b) Disclosure of information concerning any juvenile under investigation or alleged to be within the jurisdiction of the court that would reveal the identity of that juvenile is prohibited except that publication of pictures of runaways is permitted with the permission of the parents and except as provided in G.S. 7B3102.

Relevant Regulations
North Carolina Administrative Code

TITLE 10A—HEALTH AND HUMAN SERVICES
CHAPTER 70—CHILDREN'S SERVICES
SUBCHAPTER 70A—PROTECTIVE SERVICES

SECTION .0100—GENERAL

10A NCAC 70A .0113   CONFIDENTIALITY OF COUNTY DSS PROTECTIVE SERVICES RECORDS

(a) The county director shall not allow anyone outside of the county department of social services other than state and federal agency personnel carrying out their lawful responsibilities for program audit and review to examine a protective services case record as described in Rule .0112 of this Subchapter unless:

    (1)   the judge orders the county director to allow examination; or

    (2)   the child or the child's attorney requests to examine his own record.

(b) The county director in carrying out his duties may share information and a summary of documentation from the case record without a court order with public or private agencies or individuals that are being utilized to provide or facilitate the provision of protective services to a child.

(c) The county director shall allow the District Attorney or his designee access to the case record, including any information or documentation therein, which he needs to carry out his mandated responsibilities that result from a report of confirmed abuse or from the county director's decision not to file a petition.

TITLE 14B—PUBLIC SAFETY
CHAPTER 11—DIVISION OF JUVENILE JUSTICE
SUBCHAPTER 11A—DEPARTMENTAL MANDATES

SECTION .0300—INFORMATION SHARING

14B NCAC 11A .0301   DESIGNATED AGENCIES AUTHORIZED TO SHARE INFORMATION

The following agencies shall share with one another upon request, information in their possession that is relevant to any case in which a petition is filed alleging that a juvenile is abused, neglected, dependent, undisciplined or delinquent:

(a) The Department of Juvenile Justice & Delinquency Prevention;

(b) The Office of Guardian Ad Litem Services of the Administrative Office of the Courts;

(c) County Departments of Social Services;

(d) Area mental health developmental disability and substance abuse authorities;

(e) Local law enforcement agencies;

(f) District attorneys' offices as authorized by G.S. 7B-3100;

(g) County mental health facilities, developmental disabilities and substance abuse programs;

(h) Local school administrative units;

(i) Local health departments; and

(j) A local agency designated by an administrative order issued by the chief district court judge of the district court district in which the agency is located, as an agency authorized to share information pursuant to these Rules and the standards set forth in G.S. 7B-3100.

14B NCAC 11A .0302   INFORMATION SHARING AMONG AGENCIES

(a) Any agency that receives information disclosed pursuant to G.S. 7B-3100 and shares such information with another authorized agency, shall document the name of the agency to which the information was provided and the date the information was provided.

(b) When the disclosure of requested information is prohibited or restricted by federal law or regulations, a designated agency shall share the information only in conformity with the applicable federal law and regulations. At the request of the initiating designated agency, the designated agency refusing the request shall inform that agency of the specific law or regulation that is the basis for the refusal.

Chapter 5

Health Information

Most, if not all, protective services records will include information about a person's physical or mental health. A record may include, for example, a report from a hospital emergency room identifying injuries a child or disabled adult suffered. It could include information from a mental health provider or substance abuse treatment center about treatment plans for or assessments of a child's parent or caretaker. It may include laboratory test results indicating that a child, a parent, or another person has a sexually transmitted infection.

This information, like much of the other information in a social services record, is extremely sensitive. Because the information becomes part of the social services record when the department of social services (DSS) receives it, it is subject to the relevant confidentiality laws discussed in previous chapters. But because this information is health related, it may also be subject to an entirely different body of confidentiality laws—those governing medical records and health information.

This chapter will identify and explore some of the key confidentiality laws that may apply to the types of health information typically found in DSS protective services records, including

- the federal substance abuse confidentiality regulations;
- state law governing providers of mental health, developmental disability, and substance abuse services;
- state law governing communicable disease information; and
- the Health Insurance Portability and Accountability Act of 1996 (HIPAA) privacy regulations.

Each of these laws has a unique and complicated approach to protecting information. Because of this complexity, the analysis provided in this chapter is not comprehensive. Rather, it presents an overview of each area of the law and provides some tools to help DSS begin the process of determining whether particular information the agency wishes to disclose is subject to that law and, if so, whether disclosure is allowed.

This chapter does not address how DSS may obtain access to medical information from health care providers. Like the rest of the book, it focuses on disclosure of information from the protective services component to other components of the agency or to individuals or entities outside of the agency.

The Federal Substance Abuse Confidentiality Regulations

If DSS receives information from a federally assisted drug or alcohol program, DSS may be subject to the disclosure restrictions found in the federal substance abuse confidentiality regulations (SA regulations).[1] This body of federal law is triggered when certain types of programs[2] obtain specific types of information. If the SA regulations apply and are more stringent than any applicable state law, disclosure must comply with the SA regulations.[3]

It is highly unlikely that a department of social services would qualify as a program under the law, but that does not mean that DSS is relieved of any compliance responsibilities. If a program discloses information protected

---

1. 42 U.S.C. § 290ee-3; 42 U.S.C. § 290dd-3; 42 C.F.R. Part 2.
2. The term "program" is defined to include
   - an individual or entity (other than a general medical care facility) that holds itself out as providing, and provides, alcohol or drug abuse diagnosis, treatment, or referral for treatment; or
   - an identified unit within a general medical facility that holds itself out as providing, and provides, alcohol or drug abuse diagnosis, treatment, or referral for treatment; or
   - medical personnel or other staff in a general medical care facility whose primary function is the provision of alcohol or drug abuse diagnosis, treatment, or referral for treatment and who are identified as such providers.

42 C.F.R. § 2.11 (definition of "program"). This definition encompasses
   - a free-standing SA facility, such as an inpatient treatment facility or outpatient clinic;
   - a physician or therapist who specializes in SA treatment or diagnosis;
   - a part of a larger organization that provides SA services, such as a detox unit of a general hospital (but it would extend to the entire hospital); and
   - a program that does not provide SA treatment but provides SA diagnosis and referral for treatment, such as an employee assistance program or managed care company that evaluates whether a person has an SA problem and refers the person for treatment.

See 42 C.F.R. § 2.12(e); Legal Action Center, Confidentiality and Communication: A Guide to the Federal Drug and Alcohol Confidentiality Law and HIPAA 17–22 (7th ed. 2012). There is an exception for programs associated with the Veterans' Administration. 42 C.F.R. § 2.12(c).

3. 42 C.F.R. § 2.20 (providing that "no State law may either authorize or compel any disclosure prohibited by these regulations").

by the law to another person or entity—including DSS—it is likely that the federal law continues to apply to that information.

As compared to other confidentiality laws, the SA regulations are strict. Information subject to this body of law may be used and disclosed in only a few circumstances specifically authorized in the regulations. The regulations explicitly state that "unconditional compliance is required"[4] and authorize criminal penalties for "any person who violates any provision . . . ."[5] Therefore, it is important that DSS understand the scope and applicability of the law.

In order to determine whether the law applies to information received by DSS, the agency will need to answer the following two questions:

1. Is the specific type of information that DSS wants to disclose subject to the SA regulations?
2. If the information is a type that is subject to the SA regulations, is DSS required to comply with the SA regulations or other restrictions?

If, after considering the two questions above, DSS concludes that it must comply with the SA regulations for certain information, the agency must then answer the following question:

When may DSS disclose the information protected by the SA regulations?

Each of these questions is addressed in more detail below.

Is the Specific Type of Information That DSS Wants to Disclose Subject to the SA Regulations?

The SA regulations do not apply to every piece of information that a program may provide to DSS in the context of a protective services case. They apply only to

- information that identifies a patient—one who has applied for or been given substance abuse treatment, diagnosis, or referral for treatment—as an alcohol or drug abuser, directly or indirectly; and

---

4. 42 C.F.R. § 2.13(b).
5. 42 U.S.C. § 290ee-3(f); 42 U.S.C. § 290dd-3(f); 42 C.F.R. § 2.4 (authorizing a fine of no more than $500 for a first offense and up to $5,000 for each subsequent offense).

- information related to alcohol or drug abuse that is obtained by the program for the purpose of treating the abuse or making a diagnosis or referral for treatment.[6]

It is possible that DSS will have received information from an SA program that does not relate to the person's alcohol or drug abuse. For example, a treatment facility may share information about a person's schedule or routines that is unrelated to that person's substance abuse treatment. In this example, DSS could conclude that the information is not governed by the SA regulations and therefore disclosure by DSS is not subject to the requirement of that law. It is important to remember, however, that other social services confidentiality laws would continue to apply.

If the Information Is a Type That Is Subject to the SA Regulations, Is DSS Required to Comply with the SA Regulations or Other Restrictions?

DSS receives information through many *different* avenues. The agency often obtains health information from health care providers upon request because there are state laws that require disclosure in some circumstances.[7] A program that is subject to the federal SA regulations will likely not provide protected information to DSS upon request because the federal regulations

---

6. 42 C.F.R. § 2.12(a).

7. As mentioned at the beginning of this chapter, this book is not intended to address the complicated topic of how DSS may *obtain* information, including confidential health information. In general, DSS has broad authority to demand information—whether or not it is confidential—and to obtain cooperation from public and private providers in protective services cases. *See* N.C. GEN. STAT. (hereinafter G.S.) § 7B-302(e) (requiring disclosure of information in response to a written demand from DSS in the course of an assessment of child abuse, neglect, dependency, or maltreatment or when providing protective services, subject to a limited exception for information subject to the attorney–client privilege); G.S. 108A-103(a) (requiring disclosure of information about an adult who is the subject of a protective services investigation). These laws have a limited reach with respect to programs subject to the SA regulations. For example, a program may disclose information protected by the SA regulations in order to comply with the state's child protective services reporting law, but it may not disclose any such information in order to comply with the state's adult protective services reporting law. *See* 42 C.F.R. § 2.12(c)(6). After the initial report, the programs are severely restricted in their ability to comply with a demand from DSS for additional information about either a child or an adult protective services case. Mark Botts, *Confidentiality Laws Governing Substance Abuse Treatment Records*, 7–8 (child protective services), 10–12 (adult protective services) (Aug. 28, 2013) (on file with author).

do not expressly allow it.[8] Therefore, information protected by the SA regulations will likely come to DSS pursuant to either (1) a court order[9] or (2) the subject's written authorization.

If DSS receives the information pursuant to a person's authorization, the program must provide the recipient of the information the following notice:

> This information has been disclosed to you from records protected by Federal confidentiality rules (42 CFR part 2). The Federal rules prohibit you from making any further disclosure of this information unless further disclosure is expressly permitted by the written consent of the person to whom it pertains or as otherwise permitted by 42 CFR part 2. A general authorization for the release of medical or other information is NOT sufficient for this purpose. The Federal rules restrict any use of the information to criminally investigate or prosecute any alcohol or drug abuse patient.[10]

If information is provided to DSS pursuant to authorization and recipient was not provided with this notice, DSS *technically* is not required to comply with the SA regulations with respect to that information. In other words, it is the duty of the SA program to notify DSS that the law applies. In the absence of such notification, the SA regulations do not apply.[11]

As a practical matter, however, DSS officials may not always know if an authorization included the legally mandated notice. If the agency knows that information was received from a substance abuse facility pursuant to an authorization and it knows or suspects that the information is protected by

---

8. Unlike many other confidentiality laws, the SA regulations do not include a provision that allows disclosures that are otherwise required by law. In addition, there is a provision that expressly states that state law cannot compel a disclosure that is not allowed by the SA regulations. 42 C.F.R. § 2.20. Therefore, even though state law requires disclosure pursuant to a DSS request, a provider must not comply with that mandate if the information requested is also subject to the SA regulations.

9. The SA regulations create a construct for court orders that differs from other areas of the law. The regulations allow a court to issue an order that *authorizes* disclosure of information but they also require additional compulsory process, such as a subpoena or a warrant. *See* 42 C.F.R. Part 2, Subpart E.

10. 42 C.F.R. § 2.32 (requiring that this specific language accompany any written consent for disclosure).

11. 42 C.F.R. § 2.12(2)(iii) (providing that the SA regulations apply to any person who receives "patient records directly from a federally assisted alcohol or drug abuse program and who [is] notified of the restrictions on redisclosure . . . .").

the SA regulations, it would be reasonable to err on the side of caution and comply with the SA regulations with respect to that information.

In some instances, DSS will receive information from a provider after having presented the provider with a subpoena or warrant and a court order, consistent with detailed requirements set out in the SA regulations.[12] If the court issues an order authorizing the disclosure, the order must

- limit disclosure to relevant information;
- limit disclosure to those who need the information; and
- include other measures necessary to limit disclosure for protection of the patient and the patient's care, which may include sealing the record.[13]

When DSS receives information pursuant to this type of court order, it must comply with any requirements set forth in the order, including any specific restrictions related to disclosure.

When May DSS Disclose Information That Is Protected by the SA Regulations?

As mentioned above, information that is protected by the SA regulations may be disclosed only if the regulations expressly allow it.[14] Disclosure is allowed

- with patient authorization,

---

12. 42 C.F.R. Part 2, Subpart E (court orders authorizing disclosure and use). The regulations' requirements vary depending on whether the purpose for requesting the information relates to a noncriminal or a criminal purpose. In a protective services case, for example, DSS may apply to the district court for an order authorizing disclosure of information protected by the SA regulations. The application must not contain any patient identifying information and the patient, as well as the program holding the information, must receive notice of the application. *See* 42 C.F.R. § 2.64(a). The regulations set out the standards that the court must apply when evaluating such a request. 42 C.F.R. § 2.64(d). DSS would also need to issue a subpoena for those records because the court order merely *authorizes* disclosure; the subpoena is the vehicle for *compelling* disclosure. For a more detailed discussion regarding these court orders, see Bulls, *supra* note 7, at 14.

13. 42 C.F.R. § 2.64(e).

14. While the primary focus of this book is on DSS's authority to disclose information, it is important to note that the SA regulations also address *use* of information within the agency. For example, under no circumstances may DSS use the information to initiate criminal charges against the person who is the subject of the information. 42 C.F.R. § 2.12(d).

- pursuant to a valid court order authorizing disclosure, and
- pursuant to a subpoena or warrant that is accompanied by a court order authorizing disclosure.

Disclosure Pursuant to Patient Authorization

In order for DSS to disclose information pursuant to authorization, the authorization form must include specific elements, including the recipient, the purpose for the disclosure, and an expiration date or event.[15] DSS must not disclose information covered by the SA regulations pursuant to an authorization that "on its face substantially fails to conform" to any of the law's requirements.[16] If drafted carefully, authorization forms may allow information to be shared with multiple parties and for various purposes.[17]

Disclosure Pursuant to a Court Order

If DSS is presented with a court order that complies with the applicable provisions of the SA regulations, the agency may disclose information subject to those regulations. The requirements and criteria that the court must apply vary depending on whether the information is sought for criminal or

---

15. 42 C.F.R. § 2.31(a). The elements that must be included in a written authorization form are

- the program or person authorized to disclose the information;
- the person or organization authorized to receive the information;
- the name of the patient;
- the purpose of the disclosure;
- the information to be disclosed (specifically, what kind of information and how much information);
- the patient's signature (or that of a legal representative recognized by the regulation);
- the date the authorization form was signed;
- a statement regarding the patient's right to revoke the authorization, subject to some restrictions; and
- an expiration date, event, or condition for the authorization.

The regulations include a sample consent form in 42 C.F.R. 2.31(b).

16. 42 C.F.R. § 2.31(c).

17. For a discussion of the use of authorization (or consent) forms in the context of juvenile justice, see *North Carolina Juvenile Justice-Behavioral Health Information Sharing Guide* (Apr. 2015), www.sog.unc.edu/sites/www.sog.unc.edu/files/ JJBH%20Information%20Sharing%20Guide%20FINAL_4.7.15.pdf.

noncriminal purposes and whether the investigation relates to the patient or to the person holding the records.[18] For example, the district attorney may seek a court order authorizing access to information that is covered by the SA regulations and is included in the child protective services record. Before disclosing information, DSS must ensure that the disclosure complies with both the child protective services confidentiality laws discussed in Chapters 2 and 4 and the applicable requirements in the SA regulations.

Disclosure Pursuant to a Subpoena or Warrant Accompanied by a Court Order

If DSS is presented with valid compulsory process, such as a subpoena or warrant, *and* a court order authorizing disclosure, the agency must disclose information if the court order complies with all of the applicable requirements of the SA regulations.

In addition to allowing disclosure in the three situations described above, the SA regulations also allow disclosure

- in medical emergencies,[19]
- for research activities,[20] and
- for audit and evaluation activities.[21]

The regulations specifically allow "programs" to use and disclose information for these three specific purposes, but they do not clearly authorize a person or entity that *receives* information from a program, such as DSS, to make the disclosure. It is possible, however, to interpret the regulations as allowing recipients to disclose information when a program would be allowed to disclose.[22]

---

18. 42 C.F.R. § 2.64 (noncriminal); 42 C.F.R. § 2.65 (criminal investigation or prosecution of a patient); 42 C.F.R. § 2.66 (criminal or administrative investigation or prosecution of the person holding the records).

19. 42 C.F.R. § 2.51.

20. 42 C.F.R. § 2.52.

21. 42 C.F.R. § 2.53.

22. *See* 42 C.F.R. § 2.12(d)(2) ("The restrictions on disclosure in these regulations apply to . . . persons who receive patient records directly from a . . . program and who are notified of the restrictions on redislcosure . . . ."). Guidance from the U.S. Department of Health and Human Services is ambiguous but it may support this interpretation. U.S. DEPARTMENT OF HEALTH AND HUMAN SERVICES, SUBSTANCE ABUSE AND MENTAL HEALTH SERVICES ADMINISTRATION, APPLYING THE SUBSTANCE ABUSE CONFIDENTIALITY REGULATIONS (Apr. 28, 2015), www.samhsa.gov/about-us/who-we-are/laws/confidentiality-regulations-faqs.

State Law Governing Providers of Mental Health, Developmental Disability, and Substance Abuse Services

North Carolina has an expansive body of confidentiality law governing facilities that provide mental health, developmental disability, and substance abuse (MH/DD/SA) services.[23] The term "facility" is defined broadly enough to include individual providers of these services, units within a hospital, and freestanding organizations.[24] While most departments of social services would likely not be facilities directly governed by this law, they will be indirectly affected when they receive information from a facility that is required to comply.

Typically, DSS will receive information from a facility pursuant to (1) a state law requiring information sharing,[25] (2) patient authorization,[26] or (3) a court order.[27] In all three situations, the facility is required to notify the recipient of the information—DSS—that re-disclosure of the information is prohibited without patient authorization.[28]

If DSS receives this notice from a facility, the agency must have a mechanism in place for flagging the information that is protected and complying with the restriction. This could create some administrative challenges for the agency when determining which information can be disclosed from a protective services record. For example, if a researcher requests adult protective services records and the agency is considering complying with the

---

23. G.S. 122C-51 to -56; 10A NCAC Subchapter 26B.

24. The term "facility" is defined as "any person at one location whose primary purpose is to provide services for the care, treatment, habilitation, or rehabilitation of the mentally ill, the developmentally disabled, or substance abusers . . . ." G.S. 122C-3(14).

25. The MH/DD/SA confidentiality law allows facilities to disclose information when required to do so by other federal or state laws. G.S. 122C-54(h). *See, e.g.,* G.S. 7B-3100 (requiring designated agencies, including DSS, to share information in some circumstances). Note that the federal SA regulations discussed above do not have similar language authorizing disclosures that are otherwise required by law.

26. *See* 10A NCAC 26B .0200 *et seq.* (specifying requirements that apply to disclosures pursuant to authorization).

27. A facility is allowed to disclose pursuant to a court order under certain circumstances. G.S. 122C-54.

28. 10A NCAC 26B .0208 (disclosures made pursuant to authorization); 10A NCAC 26B .0304 (disclosures made without authorization).

request,[29] it would not be able to disclose to the researcher any records that are subject to the state MH/DD/SA confidentiality law.

In the research example described above, the disclosure is discretionary. If, instead of being discretionary, the disclosure is *required* by federal or state law or a court order, DSS would be able to make the disclosure without obtaining the patient's authorization. For example, state law allows a guardian ad litem appointed in a child protective services case to have access to all confidential records, including those held by a facility subject to the MH/DD/SA confidentiality law.[30] When those same records are disclosed to DSS, it is only logical that DSS be allowed to comply with the same state law mandate. Similarly, both a facility and DSS must comply with court orders compelling disclosure of information that is subject to the MH/DD/SA confidentiality law.[31]

If DSS plans to seek authorization to re-disclose MH/DD/SA information that it received from a facility, DSS should use an authorization form that complies with the requirements of the state law. The state's authorization requirements are very similar to the requirements in the federal SA regulations, but the state MH/DD/SA law does add one additional wrinkle: an authorization form may be valid for up to one year, with limited exceptions.[32] There is an exception that applies if the reason for the authorization is to disclose information for the purpose of continuing established financial benefits. In such cases, the authorization is valid until the benefits end.

The state provides an authorization form for facilities to use.[33] The law does not require others who hold this information, including DSS, to use the state-provided form. DSS must, however, ensure that any signed authorization that it relies upon to disclose information subject to the state MH/DD/SA confidentiality law "substantially conforms" to the requirements of that law.[34]

---

29. *See* 10A NCAC 69 .0502 (allowing disclosure for research in some circumstances).

30. G.S. 7B-601.

31. G.S. 122C-54(a) ("A facility shall disclose confidential information if a court of competent jurisdiction issues an order compelling disclosure.").

32. 10A NCAC 26B .0202(a) & (b).

33. NC DEPARTMENT OF HEALTH AND HUMAN SERVICES, AUTHORIZATION TO DISCLOSE HEALTH INFORMATION (DHHS-1000) (Jan. 2003), www.ncdhhs.gov/mhddsas/statspublications/Forms/form-dhhsreleaseofinfo8-29-03.pdf.

34. 10A NCAC 26B .0202(c). *See also North Carolina Juvenile Justice-Behavioral Health Information Sharing Guide, supra* note 17, at 19.

State Law Governing Communicable Disease Information

Any information that identifies a person who has or may have a reportable communicable disease or condition is subject to a state law that specifies when that information may be disclosed.[35] This law applies to everyone—public and private entities, health care providers, and others. The wide-ranging list of more than seventy reportable communicable diseases and conditions can be found in a state regulation.[36] It includes, for example,

- sexually transmitted infections, such as chlamydia, gonorrhea, and syphilis;
- vaccine-preventable illnesses, such as measles, mumps, and whooping cough; and
- other diseases and conditions, such as HIV, hepatitis, and tuberculosis.

The law allows disclosure of this information in several circumstances, but many are related to provision of health care and protecting the public health. While this law does not have a general provision that allows disclosures that are otherwise authorized or required by law, DSS will still be required to disclose information governed by this law when mandated by federal law. For example, as discussed in Chapter 3, federal law requires DSS to share certain information, including health information, with foster parents.[37] This federal mandate permits DSS to disclose confidential communicable disease information to foster parents.

The law allows disclosure pursuant to a court order, but there is a specific requirement that allows the person identified by the information to ask that the court review the information *in camera*.[38] Because the person has the right to make this request, it is reasonable to infer that the person should have some advance notice that his or her information will be disclosed. A notice requirement is not included in the statute, but DSS may want to have a policy in place requiring that either the agency or the requesting party

---

35. G.S. 130A-143.
36. 10A NCAC 41A .0101.
37. 42 U.S.C. § 671 (a)(16) (requiring a case plan); 42 U.S.C. § 675(1)(C) (health and education records that must be included in case plan); 42 U.S.C. § 675(5)(D) (requiring that health and education information be shared with foster families).
38. G.S. 130A-143(6).

provide notice to the subject of the information when asking a court to order disclosure of this type of information.

In practice, DSS should ensure that it has policies and procedures for reviewing information before it is disclosed and redacting any information that is protected by this law. If disclosure of that information is necessary, DSS or the requesting party may seek a court order as described above. If an individual or an individual's representative requests access to protective services records (see Chapter 6), DSS should redact any information about another person that identifies the person as having a reportable communicable disease or condition.

Information Subject to the HIPAA Privacy Regulations

It is possible that DSS will be required to comply with the HIPAA privacy regulations with respect to identifiable health information in a protective services record. While this is a relatively remote possibility, it is important for DSS to consider the law and take steps to address compliance if necessary.

HIPAA includes a section entitled "Administrative Simplification," which requires the U.S. Department of Health and Human Services to develop detailed regulations designed to standardize many aspects of electronic communications in the health care industry. It also includes significant requirements related to the privacy and security of health information. The HIPAA regulations apply to certain types of people or organizations, referred to as "covered entities" and "business associates."

Depending on the services provided and the relationships that exist, a county may be a covered entity or a business associate that is subject to these federal regulations. In some counties, DSS may be providing services that would be considered health care, such as having a nurse-social worker on staff who counsels foster children or a case manager who works with families. If so, it is possible that DSS—or part of DSS—will be required to comply with the federal HIPAA privacy and security regulations.[39]

39. *See* 42 U.S.C. § 1320d-1 (applicability); 45 C.F.R. § 160.103 (definition of "covered entity").

If the DSS services that trigger coverage under HIPAA are part of the agency's protective services work, the county may be able to carve that component out of all HIPAA compliance responsibilities. If the services are included in the protective services component, then a disclosure of any identifiable health information from a protective services record must comply with the HIPAA privacy regulations, in addition to all other applicable confidentiality laws.

In order to determine whether the information is subject to the HIPAA privacy regulations, a county must answer four threshold questions:

- Is the county a HIPAA-covered entity?
- If the county is a HIPAA-covered entity, has it designated itself a hybrid entity?
- If the county has designated itself a hybrid entity, has it included DSS's protective services functions within the health care component of the covered entity?
- Is the county, including the protective services component of DSS, a business associate of a covered entity?

If DSS determines that one or both of its protective services functions are in the covered health care component or if it is a business associate of another covered entity, the agency must comply with the HIPAA privacy regulations with respect to disclosing protected health information. The county must then answer a final question:

- If DSS is required to comply with the HIPAA privacy regulations, when may the agency disclose identifiable health information?

Each of these questions is discussed briefly below. While a full analysis and explanation of the HIPAA privacy regulations is beyond the scope of this book, the information below should help DSS begin the process of evaluating if and how it must comply with this additional confidentiality law.

Is the County a HIPAA-Covered Entity?

There are three types of covered entities under HIPAA:

- health care clearinghouses,
- health plans, and

- health care providers who transmit any health information in electronic form in connection with a HIPAA-covered transaction.[40]

Many, if not all, counties are covered entities because they offer some services that qualify them as "health care providers" as that term is defined by the regulation.[41] A health care provider is any person or organization who furnishes, bills, or is paid for health care in the normal course of business. The term "health care" is defined broadly as care, services, or supplies related to the health of an individual and includes the following:

> Preventive, diagnostic, therapeutic, rehabilitative, maintenance, or palliative care, and counseling, service, assessment, or procedure with respect to the physical or mental condition, or functional status, of an individual or that affects the structure or function of the body.[42]

County-based examples include child health clinics, dental clinics, emergency management services, and some case managers.

To be considered a covered entity, a health care provider must also transmit health information in electronic form in connection with a HIPAA-covered transaction. The types of transactions covered by HIPAA relate primarily to communications between and among health care providers

---

40. *See* Aimee N. Wall, *Should a Local Government Be a HIPAA Hybrid Entity?* Coates' Canons: NC Local Government Law Blog (Apr. 29, 2015), http://canons.sog.unc.edu/?p=8084. The U.S. Department of Health and Human Services developed a series of flowcharts to help individuals and entities decide whether they fall into one of these three categories. The flowcharts are available at www.cms.gov/Regulations-and-Guidance/HIPAA-Administrative-Simplification/HIPAAGenInfo/AreYouaCoveredEntity.html.

41. Counties are most likely not health care clearinghouses, which are entities (such as billing services) that process health information, converting it from a standard to a nonstandard format (or the reverse). 45 C.F.R. § 160.103 (definition of "health care clearinghouse"). Some counties operate self-funded health plans that qualify them as covered entities. 45 C.F.R. 160. § 103 (definition of "health plan"). Assuming the county identifies itself as a hybrid entity and keeps the health plan separate from the rest of the county, the health plan's status as a covered entity should not have an impact on DSS. See the following two sections for a discussion of hybrid entities.

42. 45 C.F.R. § 160.103. Health care also includes the sale or dispensing of a drug, device, equipment, or other item in accordance with a prescription.

and payers or insurers. Examples include submitting health care claims, querying eligibility for a health plan, enrolling someone in a health plan, and coordinating benefits across plans.[43]

If the County Is a HIPAA-Covered Entity, Has It Designated Itself a Hybrid Entity?

If a covered entity performs a variety of functions—some that are required to be covered and some that are not—the HIPAA regulations allow the entity to designate itself a hybrid entity, thereby limiting its compliance responsibilities to only certain parts of the entity. By definition, a "hybrid entity" is simply a single legal entity that (1) has both covered and non-covered components and (2) designates itself a hybrid entity by identifying covered health care components. In order to become a hybrid entity, a county must draw invisible lines throughout its organization identifying who will be required to comply and who will not. Once the lines are drawn, there is no requirement that the covered entity file hybrid entity designation documentation with the federal government or any other oversight body. Rather, this is an internal exercise that prepares the entity for meeting its compliance responsibilities.

The primary benefit of becoming a hybrid entity is that it limits the county's liability exposure in the event of an enforcement action related to the HIPAA privacy or security regulations. If a county is a covered entity and does not designate itself a hybrid entity, all individually identifiable health information maintained by the entity is subject to the HIPAA regulations. For example, individually identifiable information in the protective services records would be subject to HIPAA. If DSS were to disclose such information in a manner that is not allowed by HIPAA, the county would be in violation of the federal law and could be subject to an enforcement action.

---

43. The types of transactions covered by HIPAA are described in more detail in 45 C.F.R. Part 162.

If the County Has Designated Itself a Hybrid Entity, Has It Included DSS's Protective Services Functions within the Health Care Component of the Covered Entity?

The county must evaluate all of its departments, services, and functions and determine whether each one should be covered.[44] If it concludes that DSS, or a component of DSS, would be a covered entity if it were a separate legal entity, it must include it in the county's covered health care component and ensure that it complies with the applicable HIPAA regulations. After evaluating all of the functions and services in DSS, the county may conclude that it is not required to include DSS in the covered health care component. If so, it may create a hybrid entity designation that excludes DSS from the covered component.

Is the County, Including the Protective Services Component of DSS, a Business Associate of a Covered Entity?

As mentioned earlier, HIPAA not only governs covered entities but extends to cover business associates as well.[45] A "business associate" is a person or entity that uses protected health information in order to help or support a covered entity's work but is not a member of a covered entity's workforce.[46]

---

44. See Wall, *supra* note 40, for additional information about hybrid entity designations.

45. 45 C.F.R. § 160.102(b) ("Where provided, the standards, requirements, and implementation specifications [of the HIPAA Administrative Simplification regulations] apply to a business associate.").

46. A "business associate" is a person who
- on behalf of the covered entity, creates, receives, maintains, or transmits protected health information for a function or activity regulated by the HIPAA Administrative Simplification regulations, including claims processing or administration, data analysis, processing or administration, utilization review, quality assurance, certain patient safety activities, billing, benefit management, practice management, and repricing; or
- provides certain services to or for the covered entity (legal, actuarial, accounting, consulting, data aggregation, management, administrative, accreditation, or financial services) where the provision of services involves protected health information.

There are some exceptions to this definition. For example, a member of a covered entity's workforce will not be a business associate. Also, one health care provider will not be a business associate of another health care provider with respect to disclosures involving treatment. 45 C.F.R. § 160.103. There is also an exception for a government agency that is authorized by law to determine eligibility for or enroll

It is possible that the county, including the protective services component of DSS, may be a business associate of a covered entity. If so, the HIPAA regulations require that before a covered entity shares identifiable health information with a business associate, it must have "satisfactory assurances" that the business associate will protect the information and comply with other administrative requirements.[47] These assurances are typically part of a contract referred to as a business associate agreement.[48] For example, Community Care of North Carolina (CCNC) has contracted with some counties to facilitate access to health information related to children who are in foster care or are otherwise receiving services from DSS.[49] As part of that contract, the county or DSS may be identified as a business associate of CCNC. These types of business associate relationships are probably uncommon for DSS. The agency should, however, be aware of the possibility and ensure that if such a relationship exists, it complies with disclosure restrictions in HIPAA as well as the business associate agreement.

If DSS Is Required to Comply with HIPAA, When May the Agency Disclose Identifiable Health Information?

In general, the HIPAA privacy regulations allow disclosure in many more situations than the social services confidentiality laws. Therefore, when deciding whether identifiable health information may be disclosed, it would be best to begin by asking whether the applicable social services laws allow disclosure. If they do, the next step would be to determine whether HIPAA also allows it.

Is the Information Subject to HIPAA?

The HIPAA privacy regulations restrict use and disclosure of "protected health information" (PHI). PHI is defined broadly enough to encompass

---

individuals in a government health plan that provides public benefits and is administered by another government agency.

47. 45 C.F.R. § 164.502(e)(2).

48. 45 C.F.R. § 164.504(e).

49. News Release, Community Care of North Carolina, More Foster Children Get the Care They Need (Apr. 20, 2015), www.communitycarenc.org/news-release-more-foster-children-get-care-they-ne/.

practically any type of individually identifiable[50] information that is connected to a person's health. Specifically, the definition extends to individually identifiable information in any format (oral, written, or electronic) that is created or received by one of several types of entities, including health care providers, health plans, employers, and schools, and relates to

- the health of an individual,
- the provision of health care to an individual, or
- payment for health care for an individual.[51]

Interestingly, the term "health" is not defined in the HIPAA statute or regulations, but, as mentioned above, the term "health care" is defined broadly.[52] It includes not only provision of direct medical services but common social work and care management services that may be offered through DSS.

Note that the definition encompasses basic information about the provision of care to an individual. For example, the fact that a client had an appointment with a case manager who is a covered health care provider is PHI because it relates to the provision of health care to the client. In addition, any health-related information the client shared with that case manager during the appointment would be PHI, as would the information involved with billing Medicaid or another payer for the visit.

If It Is Protected Health Information, When May It Be Disclosed?

The HIPAA privacy regulations are a complex body of law that governs both use and disclosure of PHI. The regulations allow disclosure in a wide range of situations, but every type of disclosure has its own definitions, parameters, and conditions. The list below is not a comprehensive inventory of all disclosures allowed under HIPAA, nor is it a thorough analysis of each type of disclosure identified. Rather, it offers a high-level summary of some of the types of disclosures that DSS may encounter in its work. The summary list is

---

50. The HIPAA privacy regulations do not apply to health information that has been de-identified but they establish strict criteria and requirements for de-identification. *See* 45 C.F.R. § 164.502(d)(2).

51. *See* 45 C.F.R. § 160.103 (definitions of health information, individually identifiable health information, and protected health information). Some types of information are excluded from the definition of "protected health information," such as information about a person who has been deceased for more than fifty years and employment records held by a covered entity in its role as an employer.

52. *Id.* (definition of health care).

intended to prompt DSS to further explore the law and develop appropriate disclosure policies for the agency in the following situations:

- *Disclosure with written authorization.* Unless disclosure is expressly required or permitted without authorization, DSS will need to obtain written authorization from the individual or the individual's personal representative[53] before disclosing protected health information. The HIPAA privacy regulation has detailed requirements related to the content and use of authorization forms.[54] If DSS plans to use an authorization form, it must ensure that the form complies not only with HIPAA but with other applicable confidentiality laws as well.[55]

- *Disclosure for treatment, payment, and health care operations purposes.* The HIPAA privacy regulation does not require authorization for most disclosures that are made for treatment, payment, and health care operations purposes.[56] For example, HIPAA allows DSS to transmit health information to a third-party payer, such as Medicaid, without authorization. It also allows a

---

53. In short, a "personal representative" under the HIPAA privacy regulation is a person who has the authority under applicable law to act on behalf of an adult or emancipated minor in making decisions related to health care. 45 C.F.R. § 164.502(g). For an unemancipated minor, the analysis is more complicated. For most types of health care, the minor's parent, guardian, or person acting *in loco parentis* will be the personal representative. If, however, the minor has the legal authority to consent to his or her own health care, it is likely that the parent, guardian, or other person acting *in loco parentis* should not be treated as the minor's personal representative *with respect to that particular care.* For more information about this topic, see Jill D. Moore, *Consent to Medical Treatment for Minors: Overview of North Carolina Law* (Apr. 2015), www.sog.unc.edu/sites/www.sog.unc.edu/files/Consent%20to%20Medical%20Treatment%20for%20Minor%20Children%20April%202015.pdf.

54. 45 C.F.R. § 164.508.

55. Social services confidentiality laws, the SA regulations, and the state MH/DD/SA confidentiality law all require authorization forms to include certain elements.

56. 45 C.F.R. § 164.506 (allowing disclosure for treatment, payment, and health care operations); 45 C.F.R. § 164.501 (definitions of "treatment," "payment," and "health care operations"). There are limited situations where written authorization to disclose PHI for one of these three purposes will be required. *See* 45 C.F.R. § 164.508(a)(2) (limiting disclosure of psychotherapy notes for treatment, payment, health care operations, and marketing).

DSS case manager who is a HIPAA-covered health care provider to discuss treatment-related issues with another health care provider who is working with the same client without obtaining written authorization.

- *Disclosure required by law.* The HIPAA privacy regulation allows disclosures that are required by a state or federal statute or regulation or a court order.[57]
- *Reporting of abuse, neglect, and domestic violence.* Typically, DSS is the agency *receiving* reports related to abuse and neglect. If DSS needs to disclose information to another agency for reporting purposes, such disclosures are allowed by the HIPAA privacy regulations.[58] The HIPAA privacy regulations do not expressly authorize disclosing information in the context of protective services work that is necessary *after* the initial report. However, the state laws directing DSS to do this type of work likely provide sufficient legal authority to support disclosure after the initial report.[59]
- *Disclosure to law enforcement officials.* The HIPAA privacy regulations allow disclosures to law enforcement officials when required by law or court order, in response to a warrant, and

---

57. 45 C.F.R. § 164.512(a) (authorizing disclosures that are required by law as long as the disclosure "complies with and is limited to the relevant requirements" of the law). The term "required by law" is defined as "a mandate contained in law that compels an entity to make a use or disclosure of protected health information and that is enforceable in a court of law." The term includes court orders, court-ordered warrants, and subpoenas or summons issued by a court or grand jury. It does not include a subpoena issued by an attorney. 45 C.F.R. § 164.103.

58. 45 C.F.R. § 164.512(b)(1)(ii) (allowing disclosure to make reports of child abuse or neglect to government authorities authorized by law to receive such reports); 45 C.F.R. § 164.512(c)(1) (allowing disclosure to make reports of abuse or neglect of an adult or domestic violence to government authorities authorized by law to receive such reports). *See also* 42 U.S.C. § 1320d-7(b) (excepting from any preemption state laws related to reporting of child abuse).

59. *See, e.g.,* G.S. 7B-302 ("In performing any duties related to the assessment of the report or the provision or arrangement for protective services, the director may consult with any public or private agencies or individuals . . . ."); G.S. 108A-108(a) ("Any director receiving a report that a disabled adult is in need of protective services shall make a prompt and thorough evaluation . . . . The evaluation shall include a visit to the person and consultation with others having knowledge of the facts of the particular case.").

in several other specific situations.[60] One particularly relevant provision allows disclosure to law enforcement officials upon request if the information is about a person who is or is suspected of being a victim of a crime if the person either agrees to the disclosure or the person is unable to agree but (1) the information is needed to determine whether a violation of the law by someone other than the victim has occurred, (2) immediate law enforcement activity depends on the disclosure, and (3) disclosure would be in the person's best interest.[61]

- *Disclosures in judicial and administrative proceedings.* The federal regulations allow disclosures in judicial and administrative proceedings pursuant to a court order, but only if the order expressly authorizes disclosure of the PHI.[62] Disclosure is also allowed pursuant to a subpoena or discovery request that is not accompanied by a court order, but only if
  - the person who is the subject of the information has been provided notice (or reasonable efforts to provide notice have been made) and has had an opportunity to object to the disclosure, or
  - a qualified protective order[63] has been requested or is in place.

If a protective services component of DSS is required to comply with HIPAA, this provision in particular could have significant administrative implications for disclosure of health information in the context of court proceedings.

---

60. 45 C.F.R. § 164.512(f). Disclosure is also permitted pursuant to a grand jury subpoena or an administrative request (such as a summons or civil investigative demand) for identification and location purposes, if the individual has died, if there has been a crime on the premises, and to report a crime in an emergency. One particularly relevant provision allows disclosure to law enforcement officials upon request if the information is about a person who is or is suspected of being a victim of a crime if the person either agrees to the disclosure or the person is unable to agree but (1) the information is needed to determine whether a violation of the law by someone other than the victim has occurred, (2) immediate law enforcement activity depends on the disclosure, and (3) disclosure would be in the person's best interest.

61. 45 C.F.R. § 164.512(f)(3).

62. 45 C.F.R. § 164.512(e).

63. *See* 45 C.F.R. § 164.512(e)(1)(v) (specific definition of "qualified protective order").

- *Disclosure to prevent a serious and imminent threat to health or safety.* A covered entity may be able to disclose PHI if it concludes that doing so may "prevent or lessen a serious and imminent threat to the health or safety of a person or the public."[64]
- *Disclosure for research purposes.* A covered entity may disclose PHI for research purposes, but it must comply with detailed procedural requirements before doing so.[65]
- *Incidental disclosures.* Sometimes when DSS is using information or disclosing it as allowed by applicable laws, another person may overhear a conversation or see a document that includes PHI. The HIPAA privacy regulations recognize that these types of "incidental" disclosures may happen and provide that they will not be considered violations of the law as long as the entity has reasonable safeguards in place and has a policy and practice of disclosing only the minimum amount of information to accomplish the purpose of the disclosure.[66]

Not all of the disclosures allowed by HIPAA will be permitted under applicable social services confidentiality laws. That is why it is important to begin the analysis of a disclosure question with the more restrictive social services laws that are applicable to the information.[67]

64. 45 C.F.R. § 164.512(j).

65. 45 C.F.R. § 164.512(i).

66. 45 C.F.R. § 164.502(a)(1)(iii); U.S. Department of Health and Human Services, Office of Civil Rights, *Incidental Uses and Disclosures* (Dec. 3, 2002), www.hhs.gov/ocr/privacy/hipaa/understanding/coveredentities/incidentalu&d.pdf.

67. See Chapter 3, "Adult Protective Services"; Chapter 4, "Child Protective Services."

Chapter 6

Right of Access

The concepts of confidentiality of information and an individual's right of access to that information are closely intertwined. The US Department of Health and Human Services explained this connection when it issued the proposed HIPAA privacy regulations in 1999:

> Inspection and copying is a fundamental aspect of protecting privacy; this right empowers individuals by helping them to understand

the nature of the health information about them that is held by their providers and . . . to correct errors."[1]

The connection translates readily to information gathered in protective services cases, where federal and state confidentiality laws include various provisions that establish an individual's right of access. There is, however, some tension between providing access and preserving the integrity of the protective services system. This tension is particularly strong in the context of a parent's or guardian's ability to exercise the right of access on behalf of a minor child.

As discussed in Chapter 2, Section 108A-80 of the North Carolina General Statutes (hereinafter G.S.) is the foundational confidentiality law for social services programs, including protective services for adults and children. The regulations implementing that statute are found in Chapter 69 of Title 10A of the North Carolina Administrative Code (hereinafter NCAC). The Chapter 69 regulations include detailed provisions regarding the right of access. Those regulations serve as the starting point for considering the following six questions:

1. What is the right of access?
2. Who may exercise the right of access in adult protective services?
3. Who may exercise the right of access in child protective services?
4. What exceptions to the right of access exist?
5. How is the right of access exercised?
6. What if the client has concerns about information in the record?

The general right of access established in the Chapter 69 regulations must be considered together with other, more specific state laws that may modify the right. The discussion below offers answers to some questions, but it also raises several questions that county departments of social services (DSS) will need to answer when considering how to respond to requests for access.

---

1. 64 Fed. Reg. 59917, 59980 (Nov. 3, 1999). *See also* Sebelius v. Uplift Med., P.C. et al., 2012 WL 8251345 (U.S. D. Md. Aug. 30, 2012) (Memorandum Opinion) (allowing enforcement of a $4.3 million civil penalty against a HIPAA-covered entity for violating the right of access requirements). "HIPAA" refers to the Health Insurance Portability and Accountability Act of 1996. See the discussion of HIPAA in Chapter 5.

What Is the Right of Access?

A client of DSS has the right to have access to most information about himself or herself.[2] Under the Chapter 69 regulations, the right of access includes the right both to review and to obtain copies of the information.

There is some ambiguity in state law about whether the right of access to a child protective services (CPS) record for a child and the child's attorney is limited to the right to *examine* the record. The reason for this ambiguity is that some of the CPS-specific statutes governing access use only the term "examine" when granting the right of access to the child and the child's attorney but use the phrase "examine or obtain a copy" in other contexts.[3] (See the discussion of these state statutes below.)

While one could argue that a strict reading of these laws could limit the child's right of access to examination only, the result would be impractical. Such an outcome would result in allowing the parties to a CPS case and the guardian ad litem to have copies of the information pursuant to discovery while the child does not.[4] It would also be inconsistent with the more liberal right of access granted in the Chapter 69 regulations, which clearly require the right to both examine and obtain a copy.[5] Finally, limiting the right to examination only would have significant resource implications for DSS. If, for example, a child requests access and is allowed only to examine the record, the examination would likely need to occur in the presence of a DSS representative to ensure that the integrity of the records is maintained.[6] For all of these reasons, DSS may provide a child or the child's representative with copies of the information requested.

---

2. N.C. ADMIN. CODE (hereinafter NCAC) title 10A, ch. 69, § .0301.

3. *Compare* N.C. GEN. STAT. (hereinafter G.S.) § 7B-302(a1)(2), G.S. 7B-2901(b)(1), and 10A NCAC 70A .0113 (allowing the child and the child's attorney and/or guardian ad litem to examine CPS-related information maintained by DSS) *with* G.S. 7B-2901(a) (allowing specific individuals to examine and obtain copies of the court's record in a CPS case).

4. *See* G.S. 7B-700 (governing discovery in CPS cases); G.S. 7B-601 (governing the guardian ad litem's right of access).

5. *See* 10A NCAC 69 .0301. *See also* 64 Fed. Reg. 59917, 59997 (Nov. 3, 1999) (explaining that, in the context of a HIPAA preemption analysis, one law will be considered "more stringent" than another law if it provides a greater right of access to the individual).

6. *See* 10A NCAC 69 .0304 (requiring that the DSS director or a DSS representative be present when a client reviews a record).

Who May Exercise the Right of Access in an Adult Protective Services Case?

In an adult protective services (APS) case, both the client and the client's representative, such as a guardian, attorney, or other person identified by the client, may exercise this right.

The Client

According to the Chapter 69 regulations, the client may exercise this right. The term "client" is defined broadly to include

- any applicant for, or recipient of, public assistance or services; and
- someone who makes inquiries, is interviewed, or is or has been otherwise served to some extent by the agency.

It also includes someone who is "acting responsibly" on behalf of a person who falls into one of the two categories of clients listed above.

With this expansive definition, the state law has cast a net wide enough to include not only people applying for or receiving services from the agency but also *any* person who "makes inquiries, is interviewed," or is otherwise served by the agency.[7] This definition is not necessarily intuitive. Dictionary definitions of the term "client" are typically tied to providing services to an individual.[8]

This definition of client would encompass, for example, a neighbor who is interviewed about a disabled adult who was the subject of a report of abuse. By including the neighbor in the definition of client, the law is granting the neighbor a right of access, but the right is limited to information about the neighbor. In this hypothetical scenario, the right of access would likely extend only to those records that recount the interview with the neighbor. It would not extend to other information in the record about the disabled adult, caretakers, or family.

---

7. 10A NCAC 69 .0101.

8. *See* MERRIAM-WEBSTER DICTIONARY (2015), www.merriam-webster.com/dictionary/client (defining the term "client" to mean, among other things, a customer and a person served by or utilizing the services of a social agency).

The Client's Representative

In the context of the right of access, state law recognizes two types of authorized representatives: "someone acting responsibly" and "personal representatives." Both types are allowed to exercise the right of access on behalf of the client.

As mentioned above, the general definition of client encompasses the concept of "someone acting responsibly for the client."[9] This concept of "acting responsibly" is not defined in statute or regulation. Rather, the regulation relies on the agency to adopt a policy that explains when another person should be considered to be acting responsibly for a client.[10] It certainly would include individuals with whom an adult has a formal relationship, such as his or her guardian or attorney, but it could also conceivably include a family member, friend, or someone else who has a more informal caretaking role. Because this concept is captured in the definition of client and a client has a right of access, a person "acting responsibly" for the client—however DSS defines that term—may exercise the client's right of access.

The "personal representative" concept is different and is included in a different regulation. Under this provision, the client may affirmatively identify someone as a personal representative by submitting a written request to DSS asking the agency to share information with that representative. DSS is required to comply with such a request.[11] The client may ask that DSS provide the representative with access to only specific types of information. DSS must also comply with any such restrictions requested by the client.

The term "personal representative" is not defined in state law. The regulation specifically recognizes that an attorney may serve in this capacity, but a client might also look to a family member, a caretaker, or a friend to serve in this role. It is possible that a client could ask that a member of the media or an advocacy organization be allowed to act as a personal representative. Because there is no definition of the term, it would be difficult for DSS to challenge such a request.

Because these two types of representatives (someone acting responsibly and a personal representative) are exercising the right of the client, DSS must share only the information the client is allowed to access.

---

9. 10A NCAC 69 .0101(1).

10. *Id.* ("For purposes of this Subchapter, someone acting responsibly for the client in accordance with agency policy is subsumed under the definition of client.").

11. 10A NCAC 69 .0306.

Who May Exercise the Right of Access in a Child Protective Services Case?

In the area of right of access to a CPS case record, many different laws overlap and intersect. Perhaps one of the easiest ways to analyze the various laws is to focus on the right of access for these two groups:

- the child and the child's attorney; and
- the child's parent or guardian.

The Child and the Child's Attorney

A child involved in a CPS case clearly has a right of access to DSS information about the case, even before the child reaches the age of majority or is emancipated. Several federal and state laws specifically focused on CPS information address the right of access:

- *CAPTA.* This federal law applies to much of the CPS information maintained by DSS. It requires states to ensure that records are "made available to . . . individuals who are the subject of the report."[12]
- *Title IV-E.* This federal law requires DSS, when a child leaves foster care after having reached the age of majority, to provide the child with a copy of certain health and education information specified in the case plan at no cost.[13]
- *G.S. 7B-302.* This state law provides that even though DSS information must be held in "strictest confidence," it "may be examined upon request by the juvenile's guardian ad litem or the juvenile, including a juvenile who has reached age 18 or been emancipated."[14] This provision applies to all information in the protective services case record maintained by DSS.[15]

---

12. 42 U.S.C. § 5106a(b)(2)(B)(viii)(I).

13. 42 U.S.C. § 675(5)(D) (this substantive requirement is included in the definition of "case review system").

14. G.S. 7B-302(a1)(2). This provision also grants a right of access to the guardian ad litem (GAL). GALs do not need to rely on this right of access, however, because they are granted more expansive authority to access records in G.S. 7B-601(c).

15. The protective services case record DSS is required to maintain is extensive. The required contents of the record are specified in 10A NCAC 70A .0113 and described in more detail in the state manual. *See* NC DIVISION OF SOCIAL SERVICES, FAMILY SERVICES MANUAL, Vol. I, Ch. VIII, Sec. 1424, Case Record

- *G.S. 7B-2901(a).* This state law applies to court records after a petition has been filed alleging abuse, neglect, or dependency. It governs "the summons, petition, custody order, court order, written motions, the electronic or mechanical recording of the hearing, and other papers filed in the proceeding." The statute allows these records to be released to the child and the child's guardian ad litem.

- *G.S. 7B-2901(b).* This state law applies only after a petition has been filed and the court has placed the child in DSS custody or in another protective services placement. It includes language that is almost identical to that in G.S. 7B-302 granting a right of access to the juvenile.[16] This provision applies to the DSS record, "which shall include family background information; reports of social, medical, psychiatric, or psychological information concerning a juvenile or the juvenile's family; interviews with the juvenile's family; or other information which the court finds should be protected from public inspection in the best interests of the juvenile." Note that the agency "record" protected by this particular law may be more narrowly defined than the "protective services case record" that DSS is required to maintain[17] and that is protected by G.S. 7B-302.

- *10A NCAC 70A .0113.* This state regulation found in Chapter 70 of Title 10A of the N.C. Administrative Code is based on authority derived from the two state statutes described above (G.S. 7B-302; G.S. 7B-2901(b)). It requires DSS to keep CPS records confidential but allows the agency to share information with "the child or the child's attorney" if they request to examine the record. Note that the statutes, G.S. 7B-302 and G.S. 7B-2901, do not expressly authorize a child's attorney to exercise the right of access on behalf of a child, but this implementing regulation does.[18]

(Jan. 2007), http://info.dhhs.state.nc.us/olm/manuals/dss/csm-60/man/pdf%20 docs/CS1424.pdf.

16. Language in G.S. 7B-302(a1)(4) and G.S. 7B-2901(b)(2) requires a judge in a criminal or juvenile delinquency proceeding to conduct an *in camera* review before releasing confidential DSS records to a defendant or the juvenile. There is an exception to the *in camera* review requirement for records that a defendant or juvenile would already be entitled to access.

17. *See* 10A NCAC 70A .0112 (specifying the contents of the case record).

18. It seems reasonable for the regulation to extend the child's right of access to his or her attorney because the attorney is acting in a representative capacity. The

While this body of law establishes a right of access for the child and most likely the child's attorney, it does not preclude consideration of the Chapter 69 regulations. As long as those regulations can be interpreted and applied in a manner consistent with the other CPS-specific laws, they should be part of the analysis. For example, it seems reasonable to assume that an older child, such as a teenager, could identify a personal representative who is authorized to exercise the child's right of access, as discussed above.[19]

The Child's Parent or Guardian

Access to CPS information by the child's parent or guardian can be a somewhat complicated issue, particularly if the parent or guardian was possibly involved or implicated in the reported abuse, neglect, or dependency. The following three avenues of access are explored further below:

- When an abuse, neglect, or dependency action is not pending, access
  - on behalf of the child as "someone acting responsibly for the client," or
  - as the child's designated "personal representative"
- Access when an abuse, neglect, or dependency action is pending
- Access at any point in a protective services case, based on the parent's or guardian's independent right as a "client"[20]

---

counterargument is that the statutes could have expressly authorized attorneys to exercise this right, but they did not. For example, G.S. 7B-2901(a) grants a right of access to court records to parents, guardians, and custodians and also separately grants a right of access to attorneys representing those individuals. That same subsection grants a right of access to children but not to their attorneys.

19. 10A NCAC 69 .0306.

20. Note that if the parent or guardian is involved in a civil case in which DSS is not a party, such as a divorce or custody matter, the presiding judge has the authority to order disclosure. G.S. 7B-302(a1)(3); G.S. 7B-2901(b). In making that decision, the judge must determine that the information is unavailable from any other source. It is not clear how this separate statutory authority intersects with the right of access. One could conclude that this statute provides the exclusive means of access for a parent or guardian involved in these civil matters. On the other hand, one could argue that DSS may first consider whether the parent has a right of access to the information without a court order.

Access When an Abuse, Neglect, or Dependency Action Is Not Pending

State statutes provide relatively clear guidance regarding DSS's ability to share information with parties, including parents and guardians, when an abuse, neglect, or dependency action is pending (see below). The law is less clear about the right of parents and guardians to have access to protective services information maintained by DSS *before* an action is pending. If one concludes that the right of access established in the Chapter 69 regulations can and should be read in harmony with other state laws governing protective services records, there are likely some circumstances in which a parent or guardian may be able to exercise a right of access.

Access as someone acting responsibly for the client. As discussed earlier, the Chapter 69 regulations provide a client with a right of access to social services records. The term "client" includes "someone acting responsibly for the client" as prescribed by agency policy. In order to give effect to the right of access, it may be appropriate in some circumstances for DSS to treat a parent or guardian as "someone acting responsibly." For example, imagine one parent reports to DSS that another parent has abused a five-year-old child. The agency conducts an assessment but does not ultimately file a petition in the case. DSS could adopt a policy for this type of situation that recognizes that the reporting parent or possibly both parents may meet the definition of someone acting responsibly for the young child.

On the other hand, one could argue that in the above example, DSS would have to deny both parents access, because G.S. 7B-302 requires that DSS hold the information in the "strictest confidence" and allows disclosure to parents only after an action is pending, as provided in G.S. 7B-700.[21] If one were to accept this argument, however, the right of access established in the Chapter 69 regulations would be severely proscribed in the context of the majority of CPS cases, where no petition is ever filed.

When DSS is developing a policy regarding the authority of a parent to be treated as "someone acting responsibly" for a child, one important factor to take into consideration is the constitutionally protected status of the parent–child relationship. The "interest of parents in the care, custody, and control of their children . . . is perhaps the oldest of the fundamental

---

21. *See* G.S. 7B-302(a1)(5).

liberty interests" recognized by the United States Supreme Court.[22] In North Carolina, this interest is reflected in a statute that expressly grants parents the right to exercise supervision and control over their unemancipated children.[23]

There are some situations in which it is relatively clear that a parent should not be recognized as someone acting responsibly for a child, such as when a parent has relinquished a child for adoption or has had parental rights terminated. There are many more situations where DSS might conclude that it is unreasonable or unwise to treat the parent as someone acting responsibly; for example, if disclosure of the information could create a risk of harm to the child or someone else. In those instances, DSS might redact or withhold some or all of the requested information, thus requiring the parent to seek a court order.

It would be challenging for DSS to adopt a policy that specifically delineates when a parent or guardian should be able to exercise the child's right of access. It may be more appropriate to adopt a broad, general policy that affords DSS significant discretion to deny requests from a parent or guardian based on the facts and individuals involved with that particular case.

Access as the child's personal representative. As discussed above in the context of adult protective services records, the Chapter 69 regulations allow a client to identify in writing a "personal representative" authorized to exercise the client's right of access.[24] It is conceivable that DSS could receive a written request from a child directing the agency to recognize a parent or guardian as a personal representative. For example, a sixteen-year-old child

---

22. Troxel v. Granville, 530 U.S. 57, 65 (2000). *See also In re* R.R.N., ___ N.C. ___, ___ S.E.2d ___, No. 186PA14, WL 4999648 (N.C. Aug. 21, 2015) (citing *Troxel*, 530 U.S. at 68–69 ("Ultimately, the best interest of the child is the lodestar, but if parents act appropriately to protect their child, their constitutional right to rear that child is paramount."); *In re* A.K., 360 N.C. 499, 457 (2006) ("The right to parent one's children is a fundamental right, and, thus, determining the validity of a court order that could negatively impact that right is critically important.").

23. G.S. 7B-3400. In other areas of the law, parents are able to exercise the right of access on behalf of their unemancipated children, subject to some limited exceptions. For example, the law relating to child custody provides that "[a]bsent an order of the court to the contrary, each parent shall have equal access to the records of the minor child involving the health, education, and welfare of the child." G.S. 50-13.2(b).

24. 10A NCAC 69 .0306.

may be living with one parent and may ask that parent to obtain access to copies of records related to a CPS assessment that took place when she was in the care of another parent or caretaker ten years earlier. This type of situation raises questions about the child's legal authority to sign such a request, but it seems reasonable that DSS should have a policy that allows a child to designate such a representative in some circumstances.

Access When an Abuse, Neglect, or Dependency Action Is Pending

When an action alleging abuse, neglect, or dependency is pending[25] and the court has placed the child in DSS custody or in another protective services placement, DSS is authorized to share information from the record with other parties to the case, including the child's parent, guardian, custodian, or caretaker,[26] consistent with G.S. 7B-700.[27] DSS may not share with parties the identity of the reporter or any information that would "lead to the discovery of the reporter's identity."[28] The agency also may not provide information that would identify any other person if the agency determines that doing so is "likely to endanger the life or safety" of that person.[29]

---

25. Note that the action referenced throughout this section is initiated when a petition is filed by DSS alleging that a child is abused, neglected, or dependent. G.S. 7B-302(c), (d); G.S. 7B-401. There are other types of petitions that may be filed in juvenile cases, such as a petition alleging a person's obstruction of or interference with a CPS assessment. G.S. 7B-303.

26. A parent will be a party to the case unless parental rights have been terminated, the child has been relinquished for adoption, or the parent was convicted of certain criminal rape offenses that resulted in the conception of the child. A person serving as the child's guardian or custodian at the time the petition is filed will also be a party. A caretaker will be a party only if the petition includes allegations related to the caretaker, the caretaker has assumed the status and obligation of a parent, or the court orders that the caretaker be made a party. G.S. 7B-401.1. The term "caretaker" is defined to mean "any person other than a parent, guardian, or custodian who has responsibility for the health and welfare of a juvenile in a residential setting" and may include, for example, a stepparent, a foster parent, or an adult relative entrusted with the child's care. It may also include a person supervising a child's care in a residential or child care facility. G.S. 7B-101(3).

27. G.S. 7B-2901(b)(4) (authorizing DSS to share information with the parent, guardian, custodian, or caretaker as provided in G.S. 7B-700, which addresses discovery); G.S. 7B-700(a) (authorizing information sharing).

28. G.S. 7B-700(a).

29. *Id.*

The statute authorizes chief district court judges to adopt local rules or enter administrative orders governing information sharing, and many judges have done so.[30] For example, in Cumberland County, local district court rules for abuse, neglect, and dependency cases provide as follows:

- DSS will provide to the office of the guardian ad litem (GAL) a draft copy of any Child Protective Service (CPS) dictation up to the date of filing, a copy of the safety assessment and any CPS case plans in place during the previous twelve (12) months.
- DSS will redact information identifying the reporter.
- Respondent attorneys may review the documents in the GAL office and make copies of the documents.
- Respondent attorneys or GAL attorneys shall not provide copies of the dictation to their clients or other parties without permission from the court.[31]

The rules include similar provisions for medical records obtained by DSS and a slightly modified approach for records related to mental health or substance abuse.[32] Local rules governing information sharing can help create consistency and standardization for both the agencies and the families involved in these cases.

If a party would like access to information from DSS that has not been made available through local procedures governing information sharing in these cases, the party may file a motion for discovery.[33] The motion must describe the information sought and include "a statement that the requesting party has made a reasonable effort to obtain the information" through any more informal method outlined in local rules. At this point, DSS is required

---

30. G.S. 7B-700(b) (authorizing local rules). Local rules are available online at www.nccourts.org/Courts/CRS/Policies/LocalRules/Default.asp. For example, Orange and Cumberland counties have local rules applicable to discovery in CPS cases.

31. Twelfth Judicial District, District Court, Family Court Division, Juvenile Case Management Plan, Rule 10.2, at 6–7 (effective July 1, 2014), http://www.nccourts.org/Courts/CRS/Policies/LocalRules/Documents/785.pdf.

32. *Id.* at 7–8 (Rules 10.3 and 10.4).

33. G.S. 7B-700(a).

to submit the requested records for *in camera* review. The agency may challenge the motion and may also request a protective order.

Access Based on the Parent's or Guardian's Independent Right As a Client

One legal avenue for providing parents and guardians with access to some information in a child protective services record is the theory that those adults have a limited right of access that is *independent* from the child's right.

As mentioned earlier, the broad definition of the term "client" in the state's regulations includes "any applicant for, or recipient of, public assistance or services, or someone who makes inquiries, is interviewed, or is or has been otherwise served to some extent by the agency."[34] In many CPS cases, DSS provides services to both the child and the parent (or other adult), which means that both would be the department's clients. As a result, it is possible that a parent or guardian has a right to obtain access to the portion of the CPS record that relates to services provided to him or her.

Federal law lends some support to this argument. One of the primary federal laws governing CPS programs, CAPTA, requires states to have "methods to preserve the confidentiality of all records in order to protect the rights of the child and *of the child's parents or guardians . . . .*"[35] If parents have a privacy interest in some of the information held by DSS, they may also have a right of access to that information.

In the absence of clear guidance from the legislature or state regulators about the potential for an independent right of access, DSS or the NC Division of Social Services could craft a policy to provide some direction to county staff on this relatively complicated issue.

What Exceptions to the Right of Access Exist?

The right of access is not absolute. There are specific exceptions in the Chapter 69 regulations, and there are aspects of the state child protective services laws that modify in significant ways how the right is exercised.

---

34. 10A NCAC 69 .0101(1).
35. *See* 42 U.S.C. § 5106a(b)(2)(A)(viii) (emphasis added).

Pursuant to the Chapter 69 regulations, DSS is not allowed to provide access to the following:

- information that DSS is required by other law to keep confidential,[36] such as the identity of the reporter[37] or information that identifies someone who has or may have a reportable communicable disease;[38]
- confidential information originating from another agency;[39] and
- information that would breach another individual's right to confidentiality.

When responding to a request for access, DSS must review the record and determine whether any information is excepted from the right of access and, if so, redact that information.[40] If, after reviewing a request for access, DSS decides that it needs to redact information, the agency must (1) document the reason for the decision to redact and (2) inform the client about the decision.[41]

The exceptions to the right of access that apply to the client also apply if another authorized person, such as a guardian, personal representative, or parent, is exercising the right of access on behalf of the client. It is important to note, however, that a guardian ad litem appointed for a child in a CPS case has an expansive right to access information and would not be subject to these exceptions.[42]

The last exception listed above may be one of the most difficult to implement because DSS records often include information from and about other people. DSS must decide when providing a person access to information

---

36. Note that the federal substance abuse confidentiality regulations specifically "do not prohibit" patient access to "his or her own records." 42 C.F.R. § 2.23(a).

37. G.S. 7B-302(a1) (protecting the identity of the reporter in a CPS case); 10A NCAC 71A .0802 (protecting the identity of the reporter and others who have knowledge of the situation in an APS case).

38. G.S. 130A-143.

39. Note the use of the term "confidential" in this provision. If the information is otherwise public or is not confidential, it is not subject to this exception.

40. If the decision to deny access is made by a person other than the agency director, it must be reviewed by the decision maker's supervisor. 10A NCAC 69 .0303(c).

41. 10A NCAC 69 .0303. If the reason for redacting the information is that it is confidential information that originated from another agency, DSS must refer the requester to the originating agency.

42. *See* G.S. 7B-601 (guardian ad litem appointed for a juvenile).

from his or her protective services record would breach another person's right to confidentiality. For example, if a disabled adult requests access to the protective services record and that record includes detailed, identifiable information about physical abuse suffered by another person or a family member's mental health, DSS should redact any information that identifies or could be used to identify the person.

The analysis of this exception is more difficult in the context of requests for access to CPS records after a court has placed the child in DSS custody or in another protective services placement. At this point, G.S. 7B-2901(b) applies, and it specifies some of the information in the protective services record that must be provided to the child. The record must include, for example, reports of social, medical, psychiatric, or psychological information concerning the child *and the child's family.* The statute further provides that the child has a right of access to that information. One way to reconcile this state statute with the Chapter 69 regulations that require DSS to redact information that breaches another person's right to confidentiality is to take the position that the statute effectively eliminates that person's right to confidentiality *in the context* of the child's access to information about the case.

How Is the Right of Access Exercised?

The first step in the process is for a client or the client's representative to submit a request. The request may be made orally or in writing.[43] The client may ask for

- an opportunity to review the information,
- a copy of the information, or
- an opportunity both to review the information and obtain a copy.

Once the request is received, DSS must provide access "as promptly as feasible but no more than five working days after the receipt of the request."[44] For a longer record, that can be a relatively short period of time to review the record and make decisions about whether information should be redacted.

---

43. 10A NCAC 69 .0301. Because the regulation allows for oral requests, DSS should not require that requests for access be submitted in writing.
44. 10A NCAC 69 .0302.

In most cases, the client will request a copy of the record. If the client requests copies, the agency must provide those free of charge.[45] If, however, the client asks to review the information, DSS must cooperate and provide an opportunity for the client to do so. A DSS representative must be present for any such record review.[46] While this type of review may be resource intensive, agencies may find that it is a good opportunity to explain information in the record to the client or to the client's representative.

What If the Client Has Concerns about Information in the Record?

If, after reviewing the record, the client or personal representative has concerns about the accuracy, completeness, or relevancy of the information in the record, DSS must allow the person to request a change.[47] If DSS agrees with the person's concerns, the agency may amend the record by adding information and notations, but it should not delete information in the record.[48] If DSS does not agree, it must allow the person to file a statement explaining the dispute and the statement must be disclosed whenever the disputed portion of the record is disclosed.

---

45. 10A NCAC 69 .0301.

46. 10A NCAC 69 .0304.

47. 10A NCAC 69 .0305.

48. If the decision not to make the amendment is made by a person other than the agency director, it must be reviewed by the decision maker's supervisor. 10A NCAC 69 .0305.

Relevant Statutes
North Carolina General Statutes

§ 7B-302.   Assessment by director; access to confidential information; notification of person making the report.

...

(a1) All information received by the department of social services, including the identity of the reporter, shall be held in strictest confidence by the department, except under the following circumstances:

(1)   The department shall disclose confidential information to any federal, State, or local government entity or its agent in order to protect a juvenile from abuse or neglect. Any confidential information disclosed to any federal, State, or local government entity or its agent under this subsection shall remain confidential with the other government entity or its agent and shall only be redisclosed for purposes directly connected with carrying out that entity's mandated responsibilities.

(1a)   The department shall disclose confidential information regarding the identity of the reporter to any federal, State, or local government entity or its agent with a court order. The department may only disclose confidential information regarding the identity of the reporter to a federal, State, or local government entity or its agent without a court order when the entity demonstrates a need for the reporter's name to carry out the entity's mandated responsibilities.

(2)   The information may be examined upon request by the juvenile's guardian ad litem or the juvenile, including a juvenile who has reached age 18 or been emancipated.

(3)   A district or superior court judge of this State presiding over a civil matter in which the department of social services is not a party may order the department to release confidential information, after providing the department with reasonable notice and an opportunity to be heard and then determining that the information is relevant and necessary to the trial of the matter before the court and unavailable from any other source. This subdivision shall not be construed to relieve any court of its duty to conduct hearings and make findings required under relevant federal law, before ordering the release of any private medical or mental health information or records related to substance abuse or HIV status or treatment. The department of social services may surrender the requested records to the court, for in camera review, if the surrender is necessary to make the required determinations.

(4)   A district or superior court judge of this State presiding over a criminal or delinquency matter shall conduct an in camera review prior to releasing to the defendant or juvenile any confidential records maintained by the

department of social services, except those records the defendant or juvenile is entitled to pursuant to subdivision (2) of this subsection.

(5) The department may disclose confidential information to a parent, guardian, custodian, or caretaker in accordance with G.S. 7B700 of this Subchapter.

…

§ 7B-601. Appointment and duties of guardian ad litem.

…

(c) The guardian ad litem has the authority to obtain any information or reports, whether or not confidential, that may in the guardian ad litem's opinion be relevant to the case. No privilege other than the attorney-client privilege may be invoked to prevent the guardian ad litem and the court from obtaining such information. The confidentiality of the information or reports shall be respected by the guardian ad litem, and no disclosure of any information or reports shall be made to anyone except by order of the court or unless otherwise provided by law.

§ 7B-700. Sharing of information; discovery.

(a) Sharing of Information. - A department of social services is authorized to share with any other party information relevant to the subject matter of an action pending under this Subchapter. However, this subsection does not authorize the disclosure of the identity of the reporter or any uniquely identifying information that would lead to the discovery of the reporter's identity in accordance with G.S. 7B-302 or the identity of any other person where the agency making the information available determines that the disclosure would be likely to endanger the life or safety of the person.

(b) Local Rules. - The chief district court judge may adopt local rules or enter an administrative order addressing the sharing of information among parties and the use of discovery.

(c) Discovery. - Any party may file a motion for discovery. The motion shall contain a specific description of the information sought and a statement that the requesting party has made a reasonable effort to obtain the information pursuant to subsections (a) and (b) of this section or that the information cannot be obtained pursuant to subsections (a) and (b) of this section. The motion shall be served upon all parties pursuant to G.S. 1A-1, Rule 5. The motion shall be heard and ruled upon within 10 business days of the filing of the motion. The court may grant, restrict, defer, or deny the relief requested. Any order shall avoid unnecessary delay of the hearing, establish expedited deadlines for completion, and conform to G.S. 7B-803.

(d) Protective Order. - Any party served with a motion for discovery may request that the discovery be denied, restricted, or deferred and shall submit, for in camera inspection, the document, information, or materials the party seeks to protect. If the court enters any order granting relief, copies of the documents, information, or materials submitted in camera shall be preserved for appellate review in the event of an appeal.

(e) Redisclosure. - Information obtained through discovery or sharing of information under this section may not be redisclosed if the redisclosure is prohibited by State or federal law.

(f) Guardian Ad Litem. - Unless provided otherwise by local rules, information or reports obtained by the guardian ad litem pursuant to G.S. 7B-601 are not subject to disclosure pursuant to this subsection, except that reports and records shall be shared with all parties before submission to the court.

§ 7B-2901.   Confidentiality of records.

(a) The clerk shall maintain a complete record of all juvenile cases filed in the clerk's office alleging abuse, neglect, or dependency. The records shall be withheld from public inspection and, except as provided in this subsection, may be examined only by order of the court. The record shall include the summons, petition, custody order, court order, written motions, the electronic or mechanical recording of the hearing, and other papers filed in the proceeding. The recording of the hearing shall be reduced to a written transcript only when notice of appeal has been timely given. After the time for appeal has expired with no appeal having been filed, the recording of the hearing may be erased or destroyed upon the written order of the court.

The following persons may examine the juvenile's record maintained pursuant to this subsection and obtain copies of written parts of the record without an order of the court:

  (1)   The person named in the petition as the juvenile;
  (2)   The guardian ad litem;
  (3)   The county department of social services; and
  (4)   The juvenile's parent, guardian, or custodian, or the attorney for the juvenile or the juvenile's parent, guardian, or custodian.

(b) The Director of the Department of Social Services shall maintain a record of the cases of juveniles under protective custody by the Department or under placement by the court, which shall include family background information; reports of social, medical, psychiatric, or psychological information concerning a juvenile or the juvenile's family; interviews with the juvenile's family; or other information which the court finds should be protected from public inspection in the best interests of the juvenile. The records maintained pursuant to this subsection may be examined only in the following circumstances:

  (1)   The juvenile's guardian ad litem or the juvenile, including a juvenile who has reached age 18 or been emancipated, may examine the records.
  (2)   A district or superior court judge of this State presiding over a civil matter in which the department is not a party may order the department to release confidential information, after providing the department with reasonable notice and an opportunity to be heard and then determining that the information is relevant and necessary to the trial of the matter before the court and unavailable from any other source. This subsection shall not be construed to relieve any court of its duty to conduct

hearings and make findings required under relevant federal law before ordering the release of any private medical or mental health information or records related to substance abuse or HIV status or treatment. The department may surrender the requested records to the court, for in camera review, if surrender is necessary to make the required determinations.

(3) A district or superior court judge of this State presiding over a criminal or delinquency matter shall conduct an in camera review before releasing to the defendant or juvenile any confidential records maintained by the department of social services, except those records the defendant or juvenile is entitled to pursuant to subdivision (1) of this subsection.

(4) The department may disclose confidential information to a parent, guardian, custodian, or caretaker in accordance with G.S. 7B700.

(c) In the case of a child victim, the court may order the sharing of information among such public agencies as the court deems necessary to reduce the trauma to the victim.

(d) The court's entire record of a proceeding involving consent for an abortion on an unemancipated minor under Article 1A, Part 2 of Chapter 90 of the General Statutes is not a matter of public record, shall be maintained separately from any juvenile record, shall be withheld from public inspection, and may be examined only by order of the court, by the unemancipated minor, or by the unemancipated minor's attorney or guardian ad litem.

Relevant Regulations
North Carolina Administrative Code
TITLE 10A—HEALTH AND HUMAN SERVICES
CHAPTER 69—CONFIDENTIALITY AND ACCESS TO CLIENT RECORDS

SECTION .0100—GENERAL PROVISIONS

10A NCAC 69 .0101   DEFINITIONS

As used in this Subchapter, unless the context clearly requires otherwise, the following terms have the meanings specified:

(1) "Client" means any applicant for, or recipient of, public assistance or services, or someone who makes inquiries, is interviewed, or is or has been otherwise served to some extent by the agency. For purposes of this Subchapter, someone acting responsibly for the client in accordance with agency policy is subsumed under the definition of client.

SECTION .0300—CLIENT ACCESS TO RECORDS

10A NCAC 69 .0301   RIGHT OF ACCESS

Confidentiality of information about himself is the right of the client. Upon written or verbal request the client shall have access to review or obtain without charge a copy of the information in his records with the following exceptions:

(1)   information that the agency is required to keep confidential by state or federal statutes or regulations.

(2)   confidential information originating from another agency as provided for in Rule .0102 of this Subchapter.

(3)   information that would breach another individual's right to confidentiality.

10A NCAC 69 .0302   PROMPT RESPONSE TO REQUEST

The agency shall provide access as defined in Rule .0301 of this Subchapter as promptly as feasible but no more than five working days after receipt of the request.

10A NCAC 69 .0303   WITHHOLDING INFORMATION FROM THE CLIENT

(a) When the director or a delegated representative determines on the basis of the exceptions in Rule .0301 of this Subchapter to withhold information from the client record, this reason shall be documented in the client record.

(b) The director or a delegated representative must inform the client that information is being withheld, and upon which of the exceptions specified in Rule .0301 of this Subchapter the decision to withhold the information is based. If confidential information originating from another agency is being withheld, the client shall be referred to that agency for access to the information.

(c) When a delegated representative determines to withhold client information, the decision to withhold shall be reviewed by the supervisor of the person making the initial determination.

10A NCAC 69 .0304   PROCEDURES FOR REVIEW OF RECORDS

The director or his delegated representative shall be present when the client reviews the record. The director or his delegated representative must document in the client record the review of the record by the client.

10A NCAC 69 .0305   CONTESTED INFORMATION

A client may contest the accuracy, completeness or relevancy of the information in his record. A correction of the contested information, but not the deletion of the original information if it is required to support receipt of state or federal financial participation, shall be inserted in the record when the director or his delegated representative concurs that such correction is justified. When the director or his delegated representative does not concur, the client shall be allowed to enter a statement in the record. Such corrections and statements shall be made a permanent part of the record and shall be disclosed to any recipient of the disputed information. If a delegated representative decides not to correct contested information, the decision not to correct shall be reviewed by the supervisor of the person making the initial decision.

10A NCAC 69 .0306   REVIEW OF RECORD BY PERSONAL REPRESENTATIVES

Upon written request from the client, his personal representative, including an attorney, may have access to review or obtain without charge, a copy of the information in his record. The client may permit the personal representative to have access to his entire record or may restrict access to certain portions of the record. Rules .0301 through .0305 of this Subchapter shall apply.

TITLE 10A—HEALTH AND HUMAN SERVICES
CHAPTER 70—CHILDREN'S SERVICES
SUBCHAPTER 70A—PROTECTIVE SERVICES

SECTION .0100—GENERAL

10A NCAC 70A .0113   CONFIDENTIALITY OF COUNTY DSS PROTECTIVE SERVICES RECORDS

(a) The county director shall not allow anyone outside of the county department of social services other than state and federal agency personnel carrying out their lawful responsibilities for program audit and review to examine a protective services case record as described in Rule .0112 of this Subchapter unless:

(1)   the judge orders the county director to allow examination; or

(2)   the child or the child's attorney requests to examine his own record.

(b) The county director in carrying out his duties may share information and a summary of documentation from the case record without a court order with public or private agencies or individuals that are being utilized to provide or facilitate the provision of protective services to a child.

(c) The county director shall allow the District Attorney or his designee access to the case record, including any information or documentation therein, which he needs to carry out his mandated responsibilities that result from a report of confirmed abuse or from the county director's decision not to file a petition.

Appendix

Analyzing Problems Involving Confidentiality

Finding the right answer to questions involving confidentiality . . . is often difficult, and, in some instances, there may not be a clear "black and white" answer to questions involving the use, protection, disclosure, or acquisition of confidential information.

Social services agencies, however, can use a three-step process to analyze problems involving confidentiality:

1. Define the problem, question, or issue.
2. Identify the applicable law or laws.
3. Apply the law or laws to the problem, question, or issue.

Defining the Problem, Question, or Issue. The first step of the process is crucial because the other two steps depend on clearly defining the problem, question, or issue. In this step, a social services agency should determine, first, whether the problem, question, or issue involves

- a social services agency's authority to *obtain* information from another agency or individual;
- the agency's authority to *use* confidential information in its possession for purposes other than that for which the information was obtained or generated;

Reproduced from John L. Saxon, Social Services in North Carolina 232–35 (UNC School of Government, 2008).

- the agency's obligation to *protect* confidential information from unauthorized use or disclosure;
- the agency's authority or obligation to *disclose* confidential information to other agencies or individuals; or
- the right of an individual to *examine or obtain copies* of agency records that contain confidential information about that individual.

After determining the nature and context of the problem, question, or issue, the agency should ascertain the particular facts of the problem, question, or issue by asking and answering all or some of the following questions:

- What information is at issue?
- In what form (unrecorded, written, electronic) is the information maintained?
- Who has the information?
- Where is the information located?
- To whom does the information pertain?
- From what source was the information obtained?
- Who could consent to the use or disclosure of the information?
- Has consent been given?
- Can a valid consent be obtained?
- For what purpose was the information collected or obtained?
- Who is seeking the information?
- Why is the information being sought?
- For what purpose will the information be used?
- Will the information be redisclosed?

Identifying the Applicable Law or Laws. Identifying the applicable law or laws governing the collection, use, or disclosure of information in a given situation is virtually impossible without a thorough analysis of that situation. But having analyzed the situation or problem and having more clearly defined the question or issue, a social services agency should be able to identify the law or laws that apply to the situation, problem, question, or issue.

Identifying the law or laws that govern the collection, use, or disclosure of information in a particular situation, however, is much easier said than done. There are hundreds of laws governing the collection, use, protection, and disclosure of confidential information.[1] And determining whether a particular law applies usually requires a detailed legal analysis of

- the type, form, subject, and content of the information protected by the law;
- the class of persons or agencies that are subject to its requirements or restrictions with respect to the use, protection, or disclosure of confidential information;
- the class of persons whose interests or rights are protected by the law;
- the individual, governmental, and social interests or public policies that are protected or promoted by the law;
- the law's requirements with respect to protection of confidential information;
- the exceptions under which disclosure of confidential information is allowed or required; and
- the legal authority upon which the law's confidentiality requirements are based.

Applying the Law or Laws to the Problem, Question, or Issue. The third step of the process involves applying the applicable law or laws to the facts of the particular situation, problem, question, or issue.[2] Once again, though, this is easier said than done, and may require the assistance or advice of a lawyer.

---

1. Many, but not all, of the federal and state statutes and regulations governing the disclosure of confidential information by or to state and county social services agencies are identified and summarized in John L. Saxon, "An Annotated Index of Federal and State Confidentiality Laws," *Social Services Law Bulletin* No. 37 (Chapel Hill: Institute of Government, The University of North Carolina at Chapel Hill, 2002). [The index cited is not current. An updated collection of relevant federal and state laws is available online at www.sog.unc.edu/resources/tools/social-services-confidentiality-law-index.]

2. In some instances, more than one legal rule may apply with respect to the collection, use, protection, or disclosure of the information in question. And in these cases, it will be necessary to determine, with the assistance of a lawyer if necessary, which law governs the use or disclosure of information in the particular situation.

If the applicable law prohibits disclosure of the information under the specific circumstances of the problem, issue, or situation, the information may not be disclosed.[3] If the applicable law requires disclosure of the information, the information must be disclosed. And if the applicable law allows disclosure of the information, the information may be disclosed.[4] See Figure 1.

---

3. If disclosure of confidential information is prohibited, a fourth step in the process may require identification and consideration of the legal remedies or sanctions that apply to unauthorized disclosure of the information.

4. If disclosure of confidential information is allowed, a fourth step in the process requires an individual or agency to determine whether the information should or should not be disclosed.

Figure 1. Disclosure of Confidential Information: An Analytical Framework

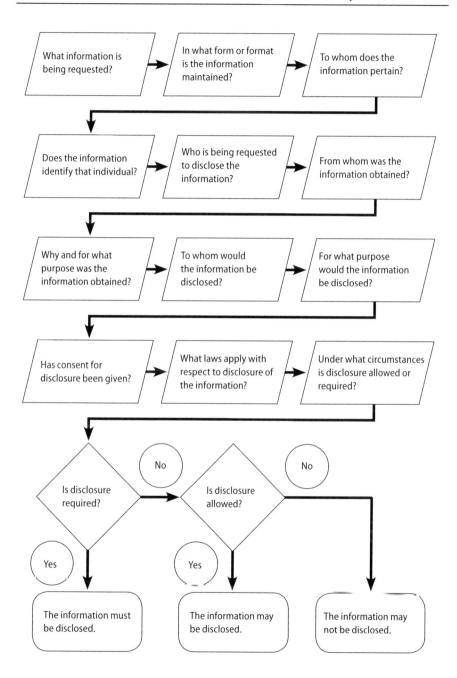